Self-healing with Body Stress Release

Unlocking Stored Tension

Gail Meggersee

dp davidphilip

Acknowledgements

I would like to express my gratitude to:
Ewald Meggersee, my partner in Body Stress Release and in life, whose difficult journey led to the creation of BSR; all the BSR practitioners who provided information on cases from their records: the BSR clients; Jane Toerien, my editor, friend and colleague, for her insight and guidance; Hally Bjarnason, my friend and colleague who drew the figures: all the BSR practitioners whose dedication and skill contribute to the upgrading of the health and lives of so many people.

Ewald Meggersee died in 2013 and Gail Meggersee in 2021,
but their legacy lives on in the training and practice of
BSR practitioners around the world.

Second edition, fifth impression 2024 by David Philip Publishers t/a New Africa Books
Unit 13a Athlone Industrial Park,10 Mymoena Crescent,
Athlone Industria 2, Cape Town 7764
South Africa

First edition in paperback published in 2007 by New Africa Books

ISBN: 978-1-4856-2305-2
e pub ISBN: 978-1-4856-2306-9

Editing: Jane Toerien
Cover, layout and design: Fresh Identity
Illustrations: Hally Bjarnason
Proofreading: Lee Smith
Photographs: Gail and Ewald Meggersee: Marinda Koen, Robin Gibbs
Printed by Amazon KDP

*David Philip is committed to a sustainable future for our business,
our readers and our planet.*

Warning: The content of this book is not intended as a substitute for consultation with a medical professional. Do not undertake any course of treatment without the advice of your doctor. The author and publishers take no responsibility for any illness or discomfort that may result from information contained in this book.

Contents

CHAPTER 1

Do you have body stress?

This book explains how body stress is a powerful factor in everyone's life, undermining health and well-being in a variety of ways. The release of body stress is a catalyst for self-healing, both physically and emotionally. People may be unaware of its presence, or misinterpret its effects, giving it some other label.

Body Stress Release is a health technique that arose out of one man's journey from debilitating pain and hopelessness back to health. When Ewald Meggersee was five years old he fell out of a tree and was semi-conscious for a week. From then on he experienced intense lower-back and leg pain, and over the next three decades numerous forms of investigation and treatment were explored but they brought no solutions. When at around the age of thirty Ewald began to experience the horror of bouts of temporary paralysis from the waist down, he had the sense that the key to his recovery lay in investigating the body's self-healing ability. This search culminated in the development of a new approach to health-care – Body Stress Release, or BSR. It is a technique that has enhanced

the lives of tens of thousands of people, and in some cases has brought about apparently miraculous life transformations. It continues to grow and is spreading around the world.

So many people live with mysterious conditions, unexplained pains, and limitations which they have come to accept as normal. They may blame their situation on the weather, or claim that their problem 'runs in the family', or is to be expected at their age. A cynical man quipped, 'If you're over sixty and you wake up in the morning without pain, you must have died in the night.'

How are you feeling right at this moment? Are you aware of any areas of your body that are tense, stiff or aching? What is your posture like? Do you feel 'at home' in your body? Are you undergoing treatment for any condition or disease?

At some stage everyone experiences health problems, which may range from mild discomfort, or vague symptoms, to diagnosed conditions. Consider which of the following four categories you fit into.

Four categories of health problems

1. *You have aches or pains or difficulties which you regard as normal for you, or inevitable considering your age, temperament or life situation.* For example, some people wake up every morning with a 'normal' headache. Older people have learned to live with their stiff knees. Anxious people expect to have aching shoulders.

2. *Your problems have been labelled as 'of unknown cause',* as medical tests and X-rays have not revealed any abnormality. Therefore you can only be offered palliative treatment, giving temporary relief. For example, anti-inflammatory medication may help reduce the pain in your leg, but the cause is not being addressed. It is particularly frightening to feel that you are at the mercy of some mysterious disease.

3. *You have been diagnosed with a certain condition,* and are undergoing treatment, but there is little or no improvement. At times you feel helpless and despairing.

4. *Your condition may have been misdiagnosed,* therefore your treatment is not aimed at the correct cause.

In each of these scenarios, a key element may be the fact that *the nervous system is being undermined in its efficiency.* In the body, just as in any organisation, communication is vital to success. The body depends on the two-way communication flow, between the brain and the cells, provided by the nervous system, in order to perform its natural process of self-healing.

To assess whether your health problems involve some disturbance of communication, see if you answer 'yes' to any of the following questions:

- Do you suffer from severe headaches that come on suddenly for no apparent reason?
- Do you get out of bed in the morning with your lower back stiff or in spasm?
- Do you experience chest pain even though your medical tests are clear?
- Do calf or foot cramps wake you at night?
- Do you have difficulty breathing although you do not have asthma?
- Do you have recurrent bouts of cystitis?
- Do you experience the sense of needing to urinate frequently?
- Do you often experience heartburn or indigestion?
- Do you wake some mornings with your hands so weak that you can barely grasp objects?
- Does 'restless leg syndrome' keep you awake at night?
- Is your posture distorted?
- Does your child have 'growing pains' in the legs?
- Does your baby cry constantly for no apparent reason?

Many mysterious problems can be traced to a logical cause – body stress. In all of the questions above, body stress may be the cause.

We all know what stress is as we deal with it every day in one form or another. But there are three facts about stress of which most people are unaware:

> Many mysterious problems can be traced to a logical cause – body stress.

- Stress is not only a mental or emotional force but may also arise from mechanical and chemical causes.
- When the level of stress goes beyond our ability to deal with it, the stress may become stored in physical structures.
- This locked-in tension, body stress, causes pressure on nerves and thereby undermines the body's communication system.

The BSR health technique has a simple and logical explanation for these situations, but it does not in any way diagnose or claim to treat any conditions. The purpose of BSR is to release the stored tension from the body, thereby activating a process that restores and enhances the body's natural ability to heal itself.

It does not use medication or machines, nor does it involve massage, manipulation, pressure points or energy meridians. It is practical and logical, and is not based on mystical concepts. BSR is a gentle technique that works in co-operation with other forms of health-care.

The information in this book is a synthesis of twenty-five years of research and practice of BSR. At times the responses to BSR appear miraculous and beyond all expectation. This simply means that miracles are natural, due to the body's inbuilt ability to heal and maintain itself. Therefore BSR has as its foundation a profound respect for the self-healing power of the body.

> ... BSR has as its foundation a profound respect for the self-healing power of the body.

To benefit fully from the body's capabilities we need to accept responsibility for our lifestyle choices and realise that we do influence our state of health.

To deny this responsibility would be to see yourself as a victim of your circumstances. This would lead you to seek an external solution and to believe that someone else will heal you. Of course outside assistance may help, but it is your own body that does the healing. When we accept responsibility we access the power that lies within us.

This book will answer these questions …

What is body stress? How does it affect your health and well-being? What is BSR? How did it come about and how does it work? Answers will be provided to questions people ask about certain puzzling experiences. For instance, in BSR practice the following situations are often encountered:

- A person may feel stiffness in his lower back when he gets out of bed in the morning, but it eases after walking around for a few minutes. As long as he goes to gym every day, his back is not painful. However, if he goes away on holiday it 'falls apart'. The pain eases when he sits with his feet up, but is worse when he stands up again. Then, just when his back seems fine, one day he reaches across the desk for a pen, and the whole back locks into a painful spasm.
- Someone may experience dizziness while reading with a book in the lap, along with strange sensations like numb fingers, a burning tongue, or a sense of something stuck in the throat when swallowing.
- A child may be fidgety, unable to sit still, and labelled as inattentive. She may complain about her sore legs, and frequently wet the bed.

This book aims to awaken a greater awareness of the wisdom of the body, and to bring hope to those seeking answers.

A story of hope and regeneration

A BSR practitioner recounts the following: 'A powerfully-built man made a huge impact on me this year. On 27th May, Barend, a forty-two-year-old truck driver, was involved in a motor accident. His second lumbar vertebra was fractured – he was paralysed on the right side, and could not use his right leg. He also lost control of his bladder and bowels. He was hospitalised for five months and underwent treatment by an orthopaedic surgeon, a physiotherapist and an occupational therapist. The fractured vertebra healed, but there was no further progress. This man, who until recently was the breadwinner for his

family, was now unable even to tie his shoelaces or control his own body functions – one can imagine the implications for himself and his family.

He heard that I practised BSR, and with the help of his family he took the initiative of having himself checked out of hospital and brought to my country town, hoping that I would work on him during the next week. As he had arranged to be there only for one week, I agreed to work on him intensively, and attended to him every day.

After two BSR sessions, Barend began to experience sensation in his right leg for the first time and he was able to sit upright for short periods. This was enough to encourage him to stay in town longer in order to have more BSR sessions. After one week, when I arrived to work on him, he astounded me – this Goliath of a man, two metres tall, was standing beside his bed. I will never forget the expression in his eyes: hope, pride and gratitude combined. He could only stand for brief periods.

After eight BSR sessions he regained control of his bladder, and after thirteen sessions he was able to use a commode. This was in the third week after commencing the BSR sessions. My new friend had reclaimed his dignity.

Then on 3rd November, my phone rang early in the morning – Barend could not wait to tell me that he had walked for the first time.'

> ... Barend could not wait to tell me that he had walked for the first time.

The sole purpose of BSR is to locate and release sites of body stress. It is not the diagnosis and treatment of any condition or illness. As it does not seek to replace any form of medical care, it is complementary to medicine.

CHAPTER 2

The birth of Body Stress Release

Ewald Meggersee's story

The history of Body Stress Release is in essence the life story of Ewald Meggersee. He was born in 1944 in the Transkei in South Africa, where his parents owned a trading store. As a small child he thrived in the freedom of the countryside, and developed a bond with the Xhosa people in the area. Then at the age of five this simple, carefree life was shattered when he fell from the high branches of a tree. When he regained full consciousness a week later he was shocked to feel a deep, burning ache in his lower back and shooting pains in his legs. The pain was unrelenting, and accompanied by other mysterious, frightening effects.

There was pressure in his bladder, as though he constantly needed to urinate, but his frequent visits to the toilet produced only a few drops.

He often woke with numb hands, with fingers that felt like stuffed sausages, and he was amazed to find that they looked normal. He would sit on his hands to try to squeeze away the strange sensation.

He was aware of a constant 'funny feeling' in the stomach which eased if he kept eating throughout the day.

When he described these strange experiences he was told it was all in his imagination. This confused him. Why would his mind lead him to create such discomfort in his own body?

School days

When Ewald started school he found it hard to sit still at a desk. He kept moving his legs to try to ease the pain and was reprimanded for fidgeting. The soles of his feet always felt bruised and at times became so hot that he feared they would burst into flames. When he ripped off his shoes and socks the teachers were not impressed by his explanation, and he was regarded as an attention-seeker.

Further inexplicable conditions followed: his breathing became laboured and he found himself panting like a dog in an effort to take in enough air. A feeling of constriction in the throat caused him repeatedly to make sounds to clear the blockage. At times an itching spread from his throat deep into his ears.

His teenage years brought even greater stress – boys are supposed to be fit, sporty and competitive. His back muscles were so spasmed that he had little flexibility. In gym class, when told to touch his toes, his fingertips could reach no lower than his knees. The gym teacher shouted, 'Boy, I told you to touch your toes!' and gave him a powerful downward push on the back of his neck. His lower back buckled and he collapsed on the floor in agony, which earned him a punishment for fooling around.

He claims to be the first boy 'dishonourably discharged' from the cadet corps at his school. Lengthy standing brought on a grinding ache in his knees which caused him to fall down suddenly. One sports day he was forced to take part in the long jump, and the landing caused an explosion of pain in his lower back.

He often felt humiliated, as at times he resembled an old man. When he went down stairs he had to cling to the handrail, anticipating his knees suddenly giving way. To stand up from a seated position, he had to press down with his hands on his thighs, to lever himself out of the chair.

No cause could be found for his problems, as X-rays appeared normal, so he was given penicillin in an attempt to cure his 'kidney pain'. One doctor pronounced his condition psychosomatic and recommended that he be taken to a psychologist. Other health problems piled up – he often

had a blocked nose and a post-nasal drip. He began to believe there must be something wrong with him mentally, as none of the other children experienced what he was going through.

Excluded from the physical activities of his peers, Ewald became quiet and introverted, focusing his willpower on suppressing the pain. He felt himself withdrawing into an emotional corner, becoming an observer of life, rather than a participant. As his outer world narrowed, he turned to introspection, and at an early age started an inner quest to find meaning beyond the physical, material reality.

Growing up and growing worse

Gail and Ewald Meggersee at university

When we met at university, I had no idea of what he was experiencing, as he never spoke of his condition. Instead, he plunged into campus activities in spite of it, playing rugby for the first time, building sets for theatre productions and exercising with weights to try to strengthen his back.

Although he was reserved, I was intrigued by his philosophical nature – his way of looking beneath the conventional surface.

Ewald graduated with a BSc degree, and I completed a BA degree and education diploma. After our marriage we moved to my home town, Cape Town, where he worked as an industrial chemist and I was a French teacher.

It became apparent that he had certain peculiarities. He wore thick socks and heavy-soled shoes to work as he said the concrete factory floor made his feet ache. He was reluctant to go swimming, even in a pool, as the cold water caused pains in his legs. Some nights I was woken by a scream of pain, and he leaped out of bed clutching his calf. He said the cramp was so sharp it felt as though his leg was broken. Never having had such an experience myself, my response was, 'Do you have to be so dramatic?'

He developed a range of allergies. Months of desensitisation treatment left him covered in the pinpricks of over two hundred injections, and then he was starved on a six week 'cleansing diet', but there were no lasting benefits.

The lowest point in our life occurred one morning when he woke feeling no sensation from the waist down.

He rolled out of bed onto the floor, pulled himself upright clinging to the wardrobe door, and hung there until feeling returned to his legs. This happened several times. Only years later did Ewald admit to me that he began to be afraid of going to sleep at night, thinking he may wake up one day permanently paralysed. He envisioned ending up in a wheelchair.

Various medical interventions were proposed – exploratory surgery to his knee cartilage to deal with his collapsing legs; having his nasal passages chiselled wider to help his breathing. Fortunately he resisted these drastic measures, having an inner knowing that the solution lay elsewhere.

A ray of hope

A friend suggested he try chiropractic. For the first time Ewald felt some hope – the spinal adjustments, two or three times a week, gave him relief from the back pain for several hours. Although he felt his back becoming even less flexible, he sensed he was heading in the right direction.

We discussed the idea of Ewald pursuing this hope by studying chiropractic himself. At first he was reluctant, as it would mean giving up his position as chief chemist of the company he worked for. We would have to

go and live in the USA for four years, as at that time there were no institutions offering chiropractic training in South Africa. Eventually it was my asking, 'Why not?' that persuaded him. These two words open up a whole world of possibilities and adventure, and sweep aside resistance. Besides, we had no children, and were free to risk creating a new life for ourselves.

In 1977 we rented out our Cape Town house and transferred to the USA, where we both enrolled in a chiropractic college in a southern state.

Becoming students again

We chose a college that was known for its 'straight' chiropractic philosophy. This promotes the principle that the purpose of chiropractic is to adjust subluxations (slight misalignments) of the spine, in order to remove interference to the nervous system and thereby assist the body in its innate ability to heal itself. As in all the colleges the curriculum included the study of pathology and diagnosis; however, the 'straight' approach maintains that the diagnosis and treatment of disease belong in the realm of medicine. The other chiropractic school of thought is referred to as 'mixer' and believes that chiropractors should include medical diagnosis and treatment of conditions in their scope of practice. However, all the chiropractic colleges are subject to the same standards – all graduates are required to pass the external examinations set by the National Board of Chiropractic Examiners.

Our years in America were financially difficult. We had sufficient funds to buy an old car and pay for our college fees and living expenses for the first few months. After that we would have to find some form of part-time employment. A new friend led us to a cottage to rent, next to a small forest. We moved in with a bed, a desk and a chair, bought from a graduating student. Ewald, a master of practicality and inventiveness, found ways to furnish the house at almost zero expense. Coming across a burned-out house, he stripped off the wooden siding, and constructed kitchen cupboards and couches. I acquired bottom dollar curtains, cushions and appliances from the Salvation Army store and 'yard sales'. We became skilled scavengers, finding discarded carpets rolled up on the pavement, and excavating damaged chairs out of dumpster bins.

It was a basic, prefabricated house, with no insulation. In winter it was freezing, so Ewald tacked thick plastic to the window frames to keep out the cold. In summer the heat was so intense we had to close all the

windows and curtains early in the morning. But Ewald's ingenuity turned it into a home. He even created an enclosed back porch so we could sit outside on sultry nights, on an old car back-seat as our sofa, safe from the vicious southern mosquitoes. The landlord was so pleased with how Ewald cared for the house that he did not increase the rent in all the years we were there.

The saga of Ewald's back took a dramatic downturn on his first day at chiropractic college. He foolishly agreed to help another student move a table, and his lower back locked up. One of the instructors saw him hobbling about, and directed him to lie on his side in the technique room. He applied an adjustment Ewald later described as being bent into a pretzel, and said, 'That's it – you can get up now.'

'No I can't,' replied Ewald, 'I can't feel my legs.' The instructor went pale – no doubt he saw a lawsuit looming. After an hour sensation returned and Ewald crawled off the bench, vowing to avoid that man's ministrations in the future.

We had hoped that the chiropractic clinic at the college would identify the source of his problems, and that his condition would start improving. We were trained in the traditional, quite vigorous spinal adjusting techniques, which often involved twisting manoeuvres. These were not suited to Ewald's spine, and his pain was escalating. He kept to himself the belief that he had made the biggest mistake of his life, coming on a wild goose chase to America. Having made so many sacrifices to be there, he felt we should stay and obtain our Doctor of Chiropractic degrees.

Paying our way

As our funds dwindled, I started to panic, as it was difficult to find part-time work in the town. 'How will we pay the college fees? I'll have to go and beg for leftover food at the back doors of restaurants.'

Ewald remained quite serene. 'We'll get jobs,' he said. 'We didn't come all this way just to give up and go home.'

The day came when I announced, 'We have fifty-six cents left.'

'That's okay,' he said, 'the jobs will come when that money's gone.'

I spent it on a packet of kidney beans and, adding the whole contents of the refrigerator, including lettuce and a cucumber, I made a huge pot of soup. We ate it every day, and by lucky chance that week we were invited

twice to dinner by friends, and there was enough petrol in the car to keep us going.

Sunday arrived – the day of zero money – and a fellow student phoned to ask if we would like to take over his job, cleaning a pre-school at night. 'I told you so,' said Ewald.

It was hard work, cleaning five classrooms, a nursery and a kitchen, every day reversing the chaos and mess caused by a horde of toddlers. Often while mopping floors Ewald would twist at just the right angle to cause him to collapse with a back spasm. This job only covered our course fees, and our next piece of good fortune came via another student. Paul, a classmate of Ewald's, asked him to join him working as a carpenter for a friend who had a small construction business. This meant being absent from college for hours each day, so I arranged for a male student to answer to Ewald's name when the attendance roll was taken. Some evenings before a test or exam, Ewald and Paul would stretch out on our homemade couches after a day's work, and I would teach them the material they had missed. My lecture was interspersed with many shouts of, 'Wake up!' as they dozed off. This novel study method paid off as they both went on to graduate with honours.

Somehow Ewald managed to survive the physical strain of the construction work, fitting siding to the wooden houses and climbing scaffolding to work on the roof timbers. He was able to block his pain mentally to the extent that the American workers were impressed by his energy, and called him 'that crazy African who lives on watermelon'. In the high temperatures of summer that was all he felt like eating, with the result that weeks after moving into their new houses the owners complained that their lawns were sprouting watermelon plants.

After our night-time cleaning work came to an end I landed a job as a waitress at a large country-style restaurant. Although I had no experience I learned quickly and the tips were good. At the end of the evening shifts I had to vacuum the carpet of my dining room. Some nights, if he was not too exhausted from the building work, Ewald would surprise me by arriving to help, lifting all the chairs onto the tables.

Ultimately we managed to go beyond survival, and saved enough money to attend some workshops, take a few vacations camping at the coast, and buy an old camper to tour the USA.

Finding a direction

Ewald's lower-back problem persisted throughout our years at the college, along with his various other complaints. We both felt that the traditional adjusting techniques we were being taught were not how we wanted to practise, not only because they had not helped him, but because we preferred a gentler method.

I embarked on a search for a different approach that would reach the core of his problems. I made a point of attending every lecture and demonstration given by visiting chiropractors, and I took several technique courses conducted off-campus.

None of these felt like the answer. Then a friend at another college sent me a pamphlet describing the method of a retired chiropractor, Dr Richard van Rumpt. He had developed a procedure for accurately 'reading' the body's muscular responses. Something went 'twang' in my awareness. A fellow student arranged for Dr van Rumpt to come and hold a weekend seminar on his technique, for twenty students, in a month's time.

The workshop cost two hundred dollars. At that time Ewald and I were only earning enough for basic living, and I had no means of finding such a large sum of money. Strangely, I was not at all anxious. I put my name down for the seminar, with a sense that it was essential for me to attend, therefore the money would come from somewhere.

Two weeks passed and I remained in this totally calm state of knowing. One afternoon our landlord appeared at the house. 'Are you using that oil heater I sold you?' he asked.

'No,' I said, 'we worked out it's going to be too expensive for us to run, so we've bought a little wood stove.'

'Well then,' he continued, 'how about selling it back to me for my Florida beach house? What did you pay me for it?'

'Seventy-five dollars,' I said.

He asked if there was any oil in the storage tank, and I told him we had recently had it filled. He said he would buy the oil from us as well, so I went to fetch the receipt from the oil supply company. It was for one hundred and twenty-five dollars. The landlord handed me a two hundred dollar bill – I had never seen one before – but I felt no surprise. I just said to myself, 'Good, here's the money for the seminar.'

During the weekend workshop with Dr van Rumpt I had a sense of 'here lies truth'. A brilliant original thinker and dedicated teacher, he was

not regarded as credible by the American chiropractic mainstream, as his approach was so different from traditional chiropractic. He taught how to test the body for subluxations – the chiropractic concept of vertebral misalignments – using a very specific leg-reflex test.

At a later date Ewald also attended one of these weekend seminars. At the time we had no idea that Dr van Rumpt would prove to be the catalyst of a new life for us – the turnaround of Ewald's health, and the start of a process that would ultimately prove to be a transforming force in the lives of so many people. We are profoundly grateful for the genius of Dr van Rumpt, and his generosity of spirit in sharing his research and wisdom.

Armed with our chiropractic degrees and anticipating a whole new future, we returned to South Africa in 1981.

Gail and Ewald, 2007

CHAPTER 3

Establishing Body Stress Release in the world

Ewald and I opened our chiropractic practices in our Cape Town house, using the technique that Dr van Rumpt had taught us. We invited friends and relatives to attend an introductory talk, persuading them to bring at least one person with them.

'How are we going to get enough patients to make a living?' I wondered.

Ewald's reply was, 'Don't worry about getting patients, worry about all the people we'll have to turn away, we'll be so busy.'

These words sounded arrogant, but they flowed from the focus that had sustained us throughout our years in America – the sense that we were in the right place, doing the right thing.

Discoveries and revelations

Although there were already many chiropractors in the area, our patient volume grew steadily during the first three months. In those days health professionals were not permitted to advertise, so practices were built entirely through personal referrals.

One day I had a young woman patient who was in intense pain and could not lie for long. I asked Ewald to work with me, to speed up the procedure. He did the leg check while I carried out the spinal tests. This proved to be a turning point. With Ewald observing the body's responses at the same time as I pressed on various points, he could detect subtle reactions,

... we were discovering lines of tension, which may be found over any structure of the body.

and he directed me to test at unusual sites and in various directions. It was a revelation, and opened up new possibilities. It also enabled us to see how different areas of the body interrelate – how one site of pressure will be present along with other specific locations. We realised we were not dealing with vertebral or other bone misalignments; we were discovering lines of tension, which may be found over any structure of the body.

We kept in contact by letter with Dr van Rumpt, who encouraged us to keep experimenting and applying our findings. Sadly, he died a few years later, in his eighties.

Ewald and I started working as a team on all our patients, and keeping detailed notes of our findings. People were intrigued by this novel procedure, which involved the two of us communicating in a code. A patient brought her children to her first appointment – a boy of five and a girl of four, who sat in silence and watched intently. At her next session she told us she had found them 'working' on their dog on the coffee table. While the girl prodded on his back, saying, 'Right, superior ...,' the boy wiggled the dog's back legs and murmured, 'Yes ... clear ... yes ...'

The practice expanded exponentially as people experienced the effects and spread the word. Within five months we were fully booked, with a waiting list for new patients, and we hired a receptionist. As the calls came in from prospective patients, she wrote down an outline of the stories they told her. Some of these were soap operas of misfortune, and

at times we were persuaded to fit in extra appointments, either during lunch break or after hours. Often at the end of the day I was too tired to cook, so we went out for dinner and continued to talk shop, dissecting the discoveries of the day. We started receiving referrals from medical doctors, both GPs and specialists, who had heard about our work from their patients. Eventually we met some of them when they came to consult us about their own conditions.

We were privileged to be invited by an orthopaedic surgeon to attend a laminectomy operation. This is performed in the case of a severely damaged inter-vertebral disc which is causing spinal nerve or cord pressure. The surgeon gains access to the disc by making a small opening in the bone, through which the bulging, shredded disc material is removed. I observed the whole fascinating procedure, although the theatre nurses had to prop me up three times when I became faint and slumped to the floor. In discussing lower-back conditions, the surgeon said he believed that the work Ewald and I were doing had the effect of helping to redistribute the pressure towards normal within a bulging, or herniated, disc.

Ewald's personal miracle

Every day was exciting, as our patients' bodies revealed their wisdom to us. The responses Ewald observed as I carried out the tests directed us to new possibilities, new 'patterns of tensions', and an appreciation of the interconnectedness of all areas. Daily we saw 'miracles' as self-healing was catalysed in people, and we came to expect them as the norm.

Ewald was the supreme guinea pig, as naturally I tested everything we learned on him. His core problem was deep compression in the lower back. As the 'layers' of tension had been accumulated over thirty years, it was a process to 'peel' these away. His lower back became more and more sensitive each time I worked on him. He told me only later that at one stage the back pain escalated so much, as feeling returned to numbed nerve pathways, that he was on the verge of telling me to stop. But one change encouraged him to see the process through – his lower back was becoming flexible for the first time in his memory.

To restrict movement during this vulnerable time, he wore an elastic binder to support his lower back. I remember a beach holiday when he sported the binder over his bathing costume and wore long rugby socks to keep his legs warm – an unusual statement in beach fashion.

No pain

One morning Ewald woke with a strange feeling of dread, a sense that something was wrong – then he realised it was because something was missing: for the first time ever he had no pain. It had taken a year to reach this point. I believe the process would have gone much faster if we had not been learning as we went along.

Soon after that momentous day we were on Camps Bay beach, where the sea temperature never rises above icy. Ewald went and stood waist deep in the water for over an hour, wearing a constant grin. He kept saying, 'This is amazing – there are no shooting pains in my legs at all!'

The pain came and went over the next few weeks, with the pain-free periods lengthening. He still had a feeling of weakness in his lower back – not surprising, as those muscles had been locked in tension for decades, and therefore had not been able to develop tone and strength. He worked with the simple exercise we recommend to people, and the day came when he stood through an entire rugby game and his back did not even feel tired.

The lower back was the focal area of his problems, but I also worked extensively on his whole spine. As pressure was released, there was upgrading of the communication of his nervous system in general, and his various mysterious ailments steadily withdrew.

Gail's health journey

The saga of Ewald's transformation is more dramatic than my story, but I also experienced profound benefits as he applied our findings to me. I had suffered from neck pain and headaches ever since a fall when I was twenty-one. Chiropractic had helped, but at times I still experienced extreme migraine-like headaches. For no apparent reason, pressure would suddenly build up at the base of my skull, and a pain wound its way like a hot wire through my left ear and eye, into my forehead. It seemed to reverberate into my brain and often made me feel nauseous. In time, by working together on so many people, we would come to discover the cause of this mysterious condition, and the solution. (See Chapter 14)

I had also been very susceptible to cold and flu viruses. As a teacher, on the first day of the school holidays I often came down with an infection. It was as though my immune system stretched its resources to keep me

going during term time, then dropped its guard the moment I could 'afford' to be ill.

As Ewald worked on me regularly, I noticed my resistance building. When patients came in with a cold or flu and apologised for risking passing it on to me, I assured them it would not happen. Over the years I have noticed that I am only vulnerable to these 'bugs' if my neck is stressed and I have been eating foods containing sugar. At the first sign of a sore throat or blocked nose, if my neck stress is released, the symptoms subside.

My neck has provided us with much research material, and we have made discoveries that have proved to be breakthroughs for people with the effects of old whiplash accidents.

Encountering opposition

In South Africa, as in the USA, there are two schools of thought in chiropractic. In the early 1980s the 'mixer' faction predominated and held the positions of power, and they were seeking to have chiropractic accepted as a diagnosing and disease-treating profession. However, the 'straight' chiropractic association had formed an uneasy alliance with them, out of necessity. The Minister of Health had insisted that the profession 'put its house in order' and speak with one voice, in order for the law relating to chiropractic to be changed.

In the early 1970s chiropractic had come under attack by the medical authorities, who had succeeded in having the chiropractic register closed, thereby preventing the profession from further growth. Negotiation with the Department of Health led to an agreement that new legislation would be passed in the mid-eighties, re-opening the register. Therefore the chiropractic leaders continued to encourage students to go overseas to obtain chiropractic degrees, and come back to practise in South Africa.

When Ewald and I appeared on the scene this was the position: the register was still officially closed, so that all the chiropractors who had graduated since its closure – about forty people – were practising 'illegally'. This was not regarded as a problem, merely as a technicality that would soon be resolved. However, it soon became clear, when we met with the chiropractic leaders, that it would be used against us, as we had studied at a 'straight' college and upheld that philosophy. They were determined that we would have no influence in the profession, especially during this period preceding the law change. Ironically, we had no intention of becoming involved in chiropractic politics, as we were happy to keep a low profile and just get on with our practice.

One morning our practice was raided by the police, as the chiropractic authorities had reported us for practising without being registered. Two detectives marched through our house, seized several record cards, and declared that our practice was now closed. When they tried to take our appointment diary our receptionist snatched it away. We were issued with a summons to appear in court. As they left, they announced to our waiting patients that if we attended to one more person it would be considered a second offence.

In spite of the shock, Ewald said, 'This makes no difference – we'll just keep on going,' and he took the next patient through to the consulting room. The next day we heard that another couple, who graduated at the same time from the same college, had also been raided and summonsed.

Ewald and I were required to report to the central police station in Cape Town. A young policewoman was assigned to take our fingerprints. She looked at me with big eyes – perhaps I did not look like the average criminal – and asked, 'What did you do?' For a moment I felt an urge to invent some outrageous crime, but I calmed down and simply said, 'I was practising chiropractic without being registered.' Her response was, 'Huh?'

As I stood there with my fingertips being rolled over the ink pad, I realised that we would be convicted of a crime and thereby excluded from the profession forever. We would lose our livelihood, have criminal records, and our lives would be ruined. The sense of injustice felt overwhelming, and for a moment I felt like curling up into an emotional foetal position. Then I rallied myself with the humorous thought that this would forever be a great story to tell at dinner parties.

Our patients gave us wonderful support, initiating a letter-writing campaign to the Department of Health. Through their connections in high places, the date of the impending court case against us was deferred several times. In spite of this constant threat hanging over us, we continued with our work. Other graduates from our chiropractic college in the USA returned to practise in South Africa. They were refused registration, but were not prosecuted.

We coped with the enormous stress by escaping to a sanctuary – a country cottage on the Garden Route, which we bought in 1984. Nestling in a green valley beside a lake, it was a haven of peace and sanity. We went there often for a week or two, or even just a long weekend, and put our energies into knocking down walls and renovating the little house. By 1985 Ewald expressed the wish to go and live in the country permanently – give up our practice and have the court case against us withdrawn. This time it was I who had the vision to keep going, and I convinced him that our work was too valuable to abandon.

The birth of Body Stress Release

In early 1988, with the latest court date approaching, we received an oblique message, via a client, to arrange a meeting with a high-up government official, who was fully aware of the injustice of the situation. He informed us that the charges against us would be dropped if we stepped out of the chiropractic profession.[1] We were advised that as long as we ensured that our practice was an independent legal entity we could continue practising our own technique.

This was the ideal solution, as our way of working on the body had moved completely away from chiropractic – we had developed a very different understanding, supported by a new vocabulary. We closed down for several months, then opened our Body Stress Release practice in a new location. We chose this name for our technique as it is simple and clear, and describes just what we do. Our practice was more successful than ever. At one stage I counted thirty-five medical doctors who were referring their patients to us.

[1] In 1997 some 'straight' chiropractors launched a campaign to have the chiropractic council register the practitioners who graduated from the college we attended. It culminated with our being offered inclusion on the chiropractic register. We accepted it as a matter of principle and deregistered the following year.

As we had received many requests to train others in our technique, we spent two years collating all our research and preparing the notes for a training course. In 1987 we ran a part-time experimental course over several months with six people who had approached us.

This brought us to a crossroads – either BSR would remain an unofficial, unregulated system, with no formal association and without responsibilities on our part, or it would be developed into a profession. These first practitioners voted for the latter option. Thus the Body Stress Release Association was formed, and a lengthy formal constitution was drawn up with all the provisos for a profession – a code of ethics, scope of practice, disciplinary procedures and educational standards. A firm of specialised lawyers approved the document and declared it not in contravention of any laws.

Two years later we expanded and upgraded the course content, and from then on conducted training courses every second year, as we were still in full-time practice.

A new life

Having grown up in the country, Ewald never lost the longing to return to living close to nature. At the end of 1996 his dream finally came true. We handed our practice over to a practitioner we had trained, and moved to our holiday cottage on the Garden Route. We had experienced such a wonderful connection with so many clients, getting to know about their families and sharing their personal stories, that it felt strange to suddenly detach. Over the next couple of years we returned to Cape Town for short periods, and Ewald continued to attend to some former clients.

Although our tiny village is located on a gravel road, six kilometres from the highway and 'off the beaten track', Ewald very quickly built a full practice. I stopped practising, but stand in for him when necessary.

In 2000 we bought the large house on the adjoining property, which now serves both as our home and the BSR Academy. We conduct the practitioner training course over five months each year, selecting a limited number of students from the applications which we receive from South Africa and several foreign countries. To focus his energy mainly on training practitioners, Ewald now limits his hours of practice, and refers new clients to other BSR practitioners in the area.

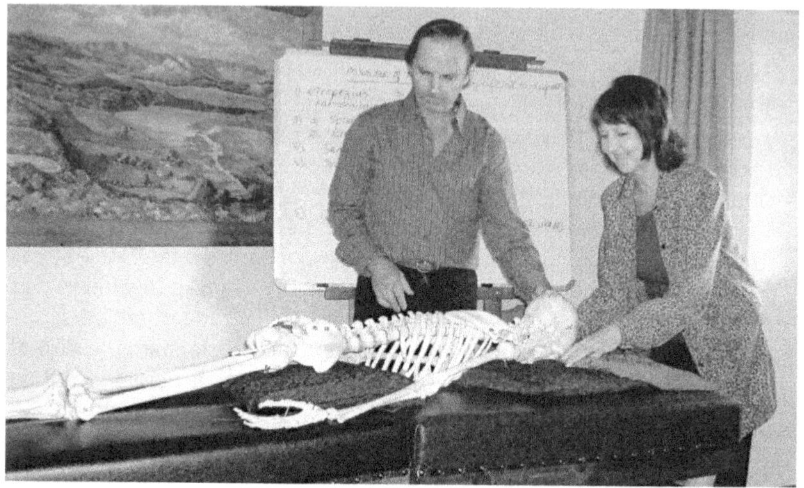

Ewald and Gail Meggersee doing a demonstration at the BSR Academy

As for his physical condition – it is as though BSR has enabled him to experience youth since the age of thirty-five. He thrives on doing heavy manual work – building, gardening and carpentry, with regular BSR releases keeping him 'in his prime'.

He has had a few serious setbacks, such as when he tripped and fell forward while holding a heavy manhole cover. It wrenched his lower back and the pain was intense. But after three days of rest and several release sessions, all pain withdrew and his back became stronger than ever.

On looking back, Ewald says he had hoped only to find something that would ease his pain. He had no idea that not only would it lead to the total recovery of his health, but that it would have such a positive impact on the lives of so many people.

We never envisioned creating a new profession, and do not recruit students – they find us, having been inspired by their BSR practitioners. We feel as though we are now at the heart of a vast network of all the people who have been helped by those we have trained. Reflecting on how it came about, we have the sense of our lives having been steered purposefully to this point. BSR owes its existence to three things: Ewald's fall from a tree, Dr van Rumpt's insight into the wisdom of the body, and the action taken against us by the chiropractic authorities.

CHAPTER 4

What is health?

To understand how body stress undermines our lives, it is helpful first to examine the concept of health. Various dictionary definitions of health include:

- One hundred per cent physical, mental and emotional well-being, and not merely the absence of disease and infirmity.
- A positive well-balanced state of mind, body and spirit.
- All parts of the body working in correct relationship to each other, all of the time.

To go beyond these concepts, we can view health as the ability to embrace fully the experience of being alive in a physical body, and to reach our highest potential of self-expression, in all aspects of our life.

To achieve this we should regard our body as our most valuable possession, and realise that health is everything and without health everything is nothing. Most of the time we only start paying attention to our bodies when something goes wrong. We need to consider what we can do to co-operate with the body in its constant striving for health, and develop an awareness of how we habitually use it. Do you bend, sit, lift and exercise in ways that respect the natural structural design of your

body? What kind of food do you give your body? Do your thoughts focus on positives or negatives? Does your environment contribute to or detract from your well-being?

Although there are many forms of health-care and many types of practitioners, ultimately we come to the conclusion that health comes from within. While health practitioners can facilitate the process of restoring wellness it is up to us to accept responsibility for our own health, and not depend entirely on outside agencies to 'make us healthy'. This involves making wise choices regarding diet, exercise, attitude, etc.

You may have heard about the fee arrangement of an oriental doctor: his patients paid him as long as they remained healthy. If they became ill, the doctor's salary was suspended until they were well again. On the surface, this may sound like a fair plan, but in fact it would allow people to abdicate all responsibility for their own well-being. It would give them carte blanche to indulge in a destructive lifestyle, and blame the effects on someone else.

Body Stress Release defines health as: *The ability to adapt constructively to the stress to which one is subjected, so that there is constant upgrading of the quality of life expression.*

The wisdom of the body

We cannot consider the human body without a sense of awe at its brilliant design, sophisticated far beyond the most intricate computer. It has been estimated that the body is composed of more than fifty thousand million cells. Groups of cells form tissues, which in turn make up organs. The organs work together in systems, e.g. the heart keeps the blood flowing through the labyrinth of blood vessels, the organs of the digestive system enable us to process and absorb nourishment, the lungs and the respiratory system allow us to breathe.

In spite of the body's complexity, all its systems and mechanisms function with efficiency and precision.

It is obvious that the body is designed to be self-healing. Unlike a machine whose parts wear out, the body is constantly regenerating itself; it is well-known that after seven years every single cell has been replaced.

Have you ever wondered how your body knows how to keep itself functioning correctly? The answer is that there is an intelligence built into it, right from the start. When the sperm fertilises the ovum, the minute cell that is formed contains a blueprint of all the cells, organs and systems that will develop and grow to maturity. We can see intelligence at work in all of nature. Think of an acorn – it contains the design of the massive future tree, complete with roots, branches, leaves and future acorns. It is like a microchip, holding all the information necessary to programme and control the growth of an entire tree.

The mystery within

A fascinating, mysterious event takes place in the fertilised embryo. Almost immediately, the single cell starts dividing, forming a cluster of identical cells that attaches itself to the lining of the uterus. Somehow, in each of these cells there is a knowing of how each must now develop and differentiate, to become the various tissues, organs and systems of the complete body, capable of performing all the complicated and intricate functions necessary for life.

What causes certain cells to become liver cells, while others form the heart, or the lungs, or the skin? In every cell there must be an awareness of its destiny, which it fulfils to perfection. To co-ordinate this process, the embryo needs a communication system.

About two weeks after fertilisation, the first system begins to form – the brain and the spinal cord with its thirty-one pairs of nerves. These spinal nerves will connect to the vast network of nerves which develops, *so that every cell of the body is in communication with the brain.*

The nervous system

We take our body's wisdom for granted, not giving any thought as to how it performs its daily miracles. In order to understand how body stress arises, and why it may have such a damaging effect on our lives, we need to take a brief look at the body's communication and control system.

Any successful business or corporation relies on an efficient two-way communication system. Without it there would be chaos. The normal functioning of the body is dependent on its communication network, the nervous system.

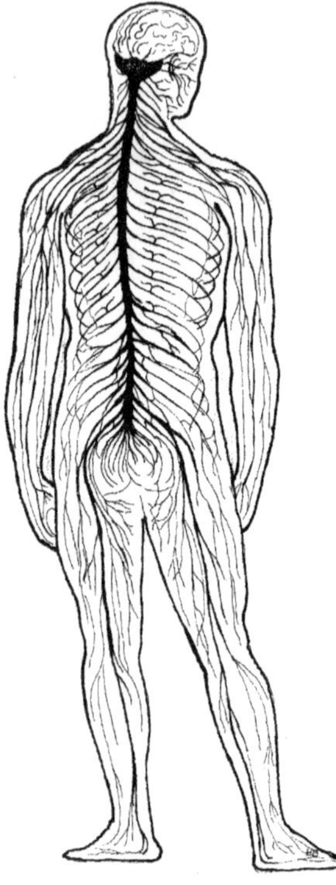

- The *central nervous system* consists of the brain and the spinal cord. The brain is enclosed in the skull and is composed of distinct parts, each responsible for specific functions. The spinal cord emerges from the base of the brain, and extends down the bony canal formed by the vertebrae of the spine. From the cord, separate nerve bundles exit through openings between the vertebrae, as the spinal nerves. These continue to branch into ever-smaller bundles, until they reach every cell of the body.
- The *peripheral nervous system* comprises the thirty-one spinal nerves and the vast network of nerves branching off them, and also includes twelve pairs of cranial nerves, which originate in the brain.

Figure 1: The brain, spinal cord, spinal nerves and major nerve pathways

Communication and control

The brain acts as the computer, processing the information brought to it by the sensory nerves, and issuing commands to the cells via the motor nerves. The *sensory* nerves bring messages both from outside the body, via the sense organs (sight, sound, touch, taste and smell), as well as from the organs and systems within. The *motor* nerves create action, both our voluntary movements, and also all those functions that occur independently of our conscious awareness. In this way the brain constantly oversees and analyses every function that is taking place, and ensures that the body adapts correctly to changing circumstances.

For example: if the temperature of the outer environment rises suddenly, the body's monitoring systems detect and convey this information to the

brain, which then directs the sweat glands to be activated, to bring about a cooling effect.

What happens when you cut yourself? The body's resident paramedics rush to the scene – platelets seal the wound and a blood clot forms, while white blood cells devour any bacteria that have entered.

If you eat too much sugar, your pancreas will secrete the hormone insulin, which causes sugar to be converted into a form that is stored in the liver, thereby lowering your blood sugar level to normal.

There is a constant flow of thousands of nerve impulses to the brain, both from the surface and from within the body, and a flow of commands from the brain to all parts of the body. This two-way communication could be referred to as the life energy flow. While this flow is normal and undisturbed, all functions will be carried out efficiently, and a state of health will be maintained.

Disrupted communication

Lillian's case is an example of widespread disturbance of nerve pathways. At the age of seventy-seven, Lillian was told that all her health problems could be ascribed to two sources – old age and 'no disc' between the fourth and fifth lumbar vertebrae.

Her whole body was hypersensitive to touch. In order to lie down she had to pile layers of soft duvets and pillows on her bed, insulating her from the pressure of the mattress. She could not lie on her left side at all. She had lower-back pain, cramping in one thigh, calf and foot, and restless legs at night. There were pins and needles in one hand, and she often experienced vertigo and headaches. Perhaps the most distressing effect was a problem she had lived with for her whole adult life – she could eat only very slowly, by taking tiny bites at a time. When she swallowed she had the sensation of the food becoming stuck before it entered the stomach.

Lillian's life story included many traumatic events, both mechanical and emotional. At ten years old she was dropped on her head, and that marked the beginning of a downhill slide in her health. She had several falls off a horse, and had been in a car accident. A number of surgeries

had been carried out – hiatus hernia repair, gall bladder removal, and a mastectomy. Compounding the physical injuries, she had suffered an extremely emotionally damaging relationship with her mother.

The BSR tests revealed sites of tension stored in the neck, the lower back, and over the ribs and the diaphragm. After the first release session there was a life-altering improvement. For the first time in fifty-five years Lillian found she could eat and swallow easily. Also, there was no more cramping in her leg, and the restless-leg condition was diminished. By the third appointment she was eating normally, and the sensations in her legs, hands and lower back had eased. Her body had very rapidly restored nerve transmission in those spinal nerves which had been compressed.

The autonomic nervous system

This term refers to specific nerves which control the automatic activities of the body – those functions over which we have no conscious control, such as movements of the digestive organs, the diameter of blood vessels, the rate of hormone secretion by glands, etc.

This system has two divisions that have opposite effects, thus together they create a state of balance. At times one will predominate over the other, as the body's needs change.

The division called the *sympathetic nervous system* activates functions necessary for 'fight or flight' – when we feel threatened, whether by a lion in the bush or by an emotional challenge. Our breathing rate increases, the heart speeds up, blood is diverted from the digestive organs to the limbs, etc. – whatever is needed to gear us up for defence. We are all familiar with the adrenaline rush of this emergency alert – even a daunting interview will cause a pounding heart and a dry mouth. The *parasympathetic* division comes to the fore for 'rest and digest', such as after a meal – the heart slows down, the blood supply to the digestive system is increased, etc.

The autonomic nervous system maintains an equilibrium that enables the body to adapt to and deal with the various forms of stress to which it is subjected.

The nerves of the autonomic nervous system

The *sympathetic* nerve fibres exit along with the spinal nerves in the chest and lower-back area, and then form a chain of about twenty clusters of nerve cells on either side of the spine. From there, nerves connect to the eyes, the other sense organs and to the internal organs. The *parasympathetic* nerves also have connections to the sense organs and internal organs, but have a different layout – some begin in the brain, and pass through openings in the skull as the cranial nerves; others arise from the lowest part of the spinal cord.

We can rely on the wisdom of the body, which uses the autonomic nervous system to take care of all the functions that keep us going, without our having to think about it.

However, when body stress becomes stored in the back or neck, the compression effect may have an impact on these nerve pathways, undermining the body's efficiency.

An example of suppressed autonomic function is that of a young woman in her twenties who was not experiencing any pain, but felt constantly tired and depressed. She was very pale, always felt cold, had minimal appetite and almost no awareness of thirst, therefore she ate and drank very little. Body stress was found throughout her neck and back. Immediately after the releases, she felt a flush of warmth course through her body. At the next appointment she said that she had developed a voracious appetite and had started cooking for the first time in her life. She also often felt thirsty and was drinking water. Her energy levels were raised and her mood had lightened.

The body is dependent on the nervous system to carry out all its functions, to maintain optimum efficiency and to heal itself. Therefore it is vital that the nerves are kept free of anything that could interfere with the transmission of nerve impulses. The presence of body stress may have a profound and far-reaching impact on the nervous system, thereby undermining health.

CHAPTER 5

Stress – what does it really mean?

Stress is a part of everyday living – the demands that life places upon us. Our body responds to stress by secreting the hormone adrenaline that prepares us for 'fight or flight', to deal with a threatening situation. The blood sugar level is raised to produce extra energy, muscles tense in order to react quickly, breathing speeds up and the heart rate increases to pump more blood to the muscles. All of these actions, initiated by the sympathetic nervous system, occur whether the stress is physical or psychological, and they are switched on automatically, before our conscious mind can analyse the event rationally.

The role of stress in our lives

Mention the word 'stress' and most people think of something unpleasant. We are constantly subjected to various kinds of stress in daily life. A certain amount is necessary, in fact essential, to our living process. It provides us with challenges that stimulate us to strive for survival and progress.

Mental stress

A mind that is not stressed or challenged by problems to be solved becomes bored and stagnates; without stimulation, intelligence degenerates – 'use it or lose it'. Anyone who has been in a job that demands less than their capabilities can relate to this – this lack of stress itself ends up being a source of extreme stress. Through mental or intellectual stress we learn new skills, develop strength and maturity, and in reaching beyond our comfort zone we experience growth and boost our self-esteem.

Physical stress

On a physical level stress is also beneficial. To maintain, develop or strengthen muscles they must be provided with the mechanical stress of exercise. Muscles waste away if a person is bedridden or a limb is in a cast for a time. Exercise improves blood circulation and strengthens the heart muscles.

Emotional stress

Emotional stress can charge us up to perform at our peak – whether we need to give a speech, compete in a sport, or cope with a demanding situation, like being at the scene of an accident. Actors say they need to feel a rush of nervousness in order to give a vibrant performance. When we find ourselves in a life situation fraught with emotional stress, such as in a relationship or in our work, we are forced to re-evaluate our life. This may lead us to set new goals and initiate positive life changes. Often when people look back at the most emotionally challenging periods or events in their life, they say, 'It was a terrible ordeal at the time, but now that I've come through it I can see how much I've gained.'

Chemical stress

When the body fights off a disease, it strengthens its immune system. If we have an adverse reaction to something we eat, we gain knowledge about what is beneficial or harmful to our body.

Adaptability

The key to understanding stress is: as long as the stress does not strain the individual, whether emotionally, physically or mentally, beyond that which he is capable of handling, it is beneficial.

> Stress must not go beyond our level of adaptability.

The stress must not go beyond our level of adaptability. Of course, this is a personal issue. Something that may stress one person beyond adaptability, e.g. a parachute jump, may be a pleasurable rush to another. There are people who seem to thrive on stress, and work best when faced with an imminent deadline. The stress sharpens their focus and creativity.

Some people discover through stress that they have underestimated their skills and strengths. A man who was retrenched in his fifties had no choice but to start his own business. The sense of achievement and satisfaction he experienced on finding he was up to the challenge led to a boost in his self-esteem. He made mental and emotional strides forward, which he would not have accomplished if he had stayed in his job.

When we manage to adapt to a stress factor (stressor), the stress is not cumulative. It is dealt with and dissipated from the body and mind. There is no 'hangover' from beneficial stress. Every time we face a challenge and overcome it, we have made a successful adaptation, which then moves us to a higher level of capability. In this way stress is our means to evolve ourselves, in all facets of our life.

However, stress becomes a negative, destructive factor in life when it goes beyond the individual's ability to adapt to or successfully deal with the stress. When this occurs, the point of stress overload is reached.

How do you react to the specific stressors in your life? This will determine whether they are beneficial or will lead to overload. Knowing yourself allows you to develop an awareness of what stretches and expands your abilities without pushing you beyond your ability to adapt.

Stress overload

When the stressful forces applied to individuals go beyond the limits of their adaptability, stress overload occurs and some outside help is needed.

Some obvious examples of severe stress overload: a bone will break if it is hit hard enough, and it needs to be aligned correctly to enable the body to mend the fracture most efficiently. If a wound is too large or deep, it must be sewn together before the body can heal it.

Stress overload may be defined as: the overriding of the body's inner, resistive powers by an outer, invasive force.

In the case of less extreme stress overload, the force or pressure to which the body is subjected may still go beyond its ability to deal with it. If the body is unable to release it, the tension becomes 'locked' into physical structures – the muscles, tendons, ligaments or other tissues remain tight and constricted, and we call this 'body stress'.

This body stress exerts pressure on nerves and disrupts communication to and from the brain and the areas supplied by the nerves involved, so normal function is undermined. Therefore the body needs some assistance to release this stored stress. *The BSR technique is designed to serve this purpose.*

People often ignore the early warning signals that they are approaching stress overload – there may be pain, extreme tiredness, a swollen joint, recurring illness, irrational thinking, etc.

The demands of life persuade people to 'keep on keeping on' and to disregard or rationalise any ominous signs. This is like disconnecting the red warning light in your car, so that it stops informing you that the engine is overheating.

A man of twenty-seven was in pursuit of the ideal of total fitness. Every day he cycled a long distance, swam several kilometres and worked out for an hour at the gym. He complained that he caught every cold and flu bug that was doing the rounds. He did not realise that his over-exercising was pushing his body into stress overload and undermining his immune system.

A BSR practitioner gives an amusing metaphor for how we suppress our awareness of imminent stress overload. She had an ancient washing machine which had served her family well for many years, in spite of the fact that she frequently put too large a load in it. As its parts wore, it began to shudder and make clanking noises. Eventually, during the spin cycle the machine shook so violently that she had to sit on top of it, to stop it from bouncing around the room. The day came when it expired with a grinding of metal and a puff of smoke, beyond repair.

When the body is stressed beyond the limit of its ability, it enters a process of making repeated negative adaptations, and therefore deteriorates. We need to address the stress overload before it leads to malfunction and possible illness and damage to tissues and organs.

Mechanical, chemical and mental or emotional stress

Most people think of stress as something that happens on a mental or emotional level. In fact, it is not 'all in the mind' – it may also be mechanical or chemical.

Mental or emotional stress

We live in an aggressive, fear-filled society, and are constantly subjected to mental and emotional pressures – anxiety about the future, financial worries, competition in the workplace, disintegrating family relationships. A study has been done to rate the intensity of various mental stress factors. Examples from the Homes-Rahe stress scale (from the *World Almanac and Book of Facts*, 1990; Marc S Hoffman, Ed.) are a score of

100 for the death of a spouse, 45 for retirement, taking out a major loan 31, going on holiday 13. In assessing various life events, the scale predicts that if a person clocks up a score of over 300 in a year, he or she has a 79 per cent chance of becoming seriously ill.

A mental or emotional stressor may be mild, e.g. irritation or impatience when things do not go as we expected. Or the tension may be stronger, as in the apprehension felt before a dreaded event. Then there is the extreme emotional stress of devastating occurrences, like grief at the loss of a loved one, or despair at a career setback.

Emotional stress may take the form of short-lived, violent feelings, like anger or sudden shock. Or we may undergo milder but ongoing mental strain, such as constant anxiety, depression, boredom or resentment.

Most people do not realise that our thoughts can have a powerful impact on the body. At times we may be aware of how we are reacting physically to emotional stress. For instance, when driving in heavy traffic, you may notice how you hunch your shoulders and tighten your neck muscles in a defensive posture, while gripping the steering wheel. When faced with a confrontation with someone, you experience 'butterflies in the stomach' and tense your abdominal muscles. When angry, you may find yourself tightening your jaw and clenching your fists.

Science has confirmed that the mind–body connection is a physical reality – emotions have an impact on our biochemistry. *In time the emotions become locked into the physical structures as body stress, resulting in constriction of the life energy flow.*

Nail-biting tension

At the age of forty-four, Conrad was at the mid-life crisis stage. He felt crushed by responsibility, with his business running into financial difficulties. His mental and emotional stress was accompanied by a stiff, aching neck and frequent headaches. He had pins and needles in his arms and his toes cramped at night. His GP diagnosed his problems simply as 'stress'.

Conrad had fractured three thoracic vertebrae in a motorbike accident in the past. Body stress was released in that area, as well as

in his neck, lower back and diaphragm. His physical problems were reduced after two sessions. In addition he had let go of a great deal of his emotional stress. This was proven by an unexpected benefit – after forty years of biting his fingernails he dropped the habit entirely.

Career stress

The life of a stockbroker involves daily, unrelenting mental stress. While many of his colleagues turned to alcohol or drugs to cope with the pressures, Geoffrey, at fifty-one, pushed himself into vigorous sports. Finally intense pain in his lower legs forced him to give up playing squash, and for three years he was unable to do anything strenuous. A neurologist detected 'some evidence of abnormality' in the calf muscles, but a biopsy showed nothing unusual. The BSR checks found compression centred in his neck and lower back, and over four months of being attended to the leg pain gradually withdrew. With a greater awareness of how his reaction to job stress was affecting him, Geoffrey has become more relaxed, and less driven in work and play.

A teacher commented on the change in posture he sees occurring in most children. Up to the age of about twelve, healthy children have straight spines. But as they approach puberty they start to become self-conscious and feel insecure in the face of new challenges. As a protective mechanism they pull their shoulders forward and contract their chests. This 'armouring' of the muscles keeps the body in a state of constant and increasing tension which, if not released, may lead to permanent postural distortions.

Mechanical stress

Fortunately our bodies are wonderfully designed to deal with the rough and tumble of life. We cannot live our lives packed in imaginary cotton wool; at some stage we all slip and fall, strain muscles, or have accidents of various kinds.

The vertebrae of the spine are connected by cartilage discs with a gel-like centre, and these compress as we move, providing flexibility and acting as shock absorbers. Throughout the skeleton, the bones are joined together by fluid-filled synovial capsules and/or cartilage pads that absorb pressure and jarring forces.

Mechanical stress may be violent and occur suddenly, as in a car accident or a fall. If the force goes beyond the body's ability to adapt to it, the tension will lock into body structures immediately, e.g. neck spasm in a whiplash accident; lower-back pain after a fall; a 'seized-up' wrist after wrenching open a jar.

Or the stress may be mild and applied over a long period of time, e.g. constantly sitting incorrectly, or repeating harmful exercises. In this case, the body stress builds up gradually. Repetitive Strain Injury (RSI) is becoming more common in people using electronic equipment.

Many people have 'minor' backache or occasional stiffness, which they ignore. They do not realise that the deep muscles in the back may be guarding and partly numbing some pressure on the spinal nerves. Then one day they may make an unusual movement that overrides the holding capability of the protective muscles, and all the muscle layers go into an instant spasm.

Rose is in her late thirties, a dancing teacher who is very active and regards herself as perfectly fit. Her back sent her a powerful message one morning: as she was waxing her legs, she bent to remove the wax strip and her back locked up. She remained doubled over, in intense pain. Her husband had to transport her to his BSR practitioner with her propped up between her two children on the back of his pick-up truck. As she could not lie down, the releases were carried out with her standing, bent over. Within a few minutes she was able to straighten up. Her lower back was extremely painful for a few days, as feeling flooded into areas that may have been compressed for years, but the pain disappeared after three sessions. Now if she feels an ache in her shoulder blade, she recognises it as a sign that tension is building up in her lower spine, and she goes for a BSR maintenance check.

In our BSR practice we have been told about some unusual causes of mechanical stress. A woman attempted to break into her own house, having forgotten her key. She managed to climb up to a small open window, but became stuck halfway while pushing herself through. A neighbour assumed her dangling legs belonged to a burglar and called the police. She suffered the humiliation of being pulled back out, the embarrassment of explaining herself, and the pain of lower-back body stress.

Another client was running to catch a train, with her shoulder bag flying out behind her. A man running in the opposite direction caught his arm in the straps, and his momentum combined with hers set them spinning in circles like a top. Eventually he gasped, 'Please, lady, let me go – I've got a train to catch.' She saw the humour in the encounter even though it left her with a stressed neck and shoulder.

Chemical stress

There is a growing silent and invisible epidemic, due to the chemicalisation of our modern world. Most people are unaware of the presence of chemical stress in their lives, yet the impact may be devastating and debilitating. (This topic is of such vital importance that Chapter 14 focuses on chemical stress.)

Every day we are exposed to substances which may be harmful, even toxic. People vary in their sensitivity to different chemicals, e.g. one person may seem unaffected by insecticide sprayed in a room while another may have a severe reaction with an immediate headache and nausea.

> When the body cannot deal with the chemical, there is an automatic tightening of muscles in a specific area of the spine.

When the body cannot deal with the chemical, there is an automatic tightening of muscles in a specific area of the spine.

Three categories of chemical stress

We may be affected by chemicals that we swallow, breathe in, or touch.

Ingestion

This refers to what we eat and drink.

- Very commonly, chemicals are added to foods, such as preservatives, colourants and flavourants. In some countries certain additives are still used which were banned decades ago elsewhere.
- There may be insecticide residue on fruits and vegetables.
- For some people, chemical stress may be the result of an intolerance or allergy to certain foods. Something may look good, it may taste great, but it may lead to stress overload.
- A poor diet is also a form of chemical stress – the body lacks the nutrients necessary to carry out its normal functions efficiently.

Inhalation

When we breathe in a harmful chemical, it is rapidly absorbed into the blood vessels in the lungs, so there may be an instant defensive, tightening reaction from the body.

Some substances are obviously toxic, such as insecticides. You may suspect others of being harmful because of their strong odour, like paints, varnishes and glues.

A woman in her thirties was experiencing almost constant headaches and tightness of the neck muscles. The practitioner detected the typical tension patterns indicating chemical stress. After three BSR sessions the pain decreased for a few days, then surged back up again to the original intensity. When all the pain withdrew after the fourth session, the client speculated that the chemical source could be carpet glue – the offices where she worked as a secretary were being refurbished. Two months later the chemical stress effects reoccurred. She explained that new carpets were being laid on another floor of the building, and the fumes were reaching her office. The resultant body stress had to be released on three occasions while the redecorating was completed.

Then there is the vast array of chemical concoctions which actually smell good – perfumes, cleaning products, air fresheners, etc. Some of these may contain substances which cause a severe stress reaction in certain people, who do not realise that their favourite product is making them ill.

Has this ever happened to you? An advertisement appears in a magazine in the form of a page impregnated with the scent of a new cosmetic or laundry product. While reading the magazine you develop a bad headache, which lessens only after you throw away the magazine. Be warned: don't buy that product.

Contact

We may absorb chemicals through the skin and experience a stress overload response.

The substance causing the problem may be something we use on the skin, like cosmetics, deodorants, soaps, etc. A new bath soap was promoted by a sample being placed in house postboxes in the suburbs surrounding our practice. That week we had a stream of clients complaining of headaches and neck pressure, and they confirmed that they were using the free gift.

We may come into contact with chemicals while using products like cleaning materials, paints, flea powder, etc. A woman 'coincidentally' had headaches every time her dog returned from the doggie parlour – she absorbed the chemicals in the anti-flea shampoo from his fur when she touched him.

Note: a product may be labelled natural or herbal, and still contain substances that cause a stress reaction in some people.

In the case of chemical stress through contact, you may use a product over a period of time, and only experience the stress effect once the substance has built up in your system to reach overload level. So a face cream you have used for weeks may be the cause of a sudden onset of headaches.

Besides these three sources of chemical stress – ingestion, inhalation and contact – it may also arise through injection, or within the body, from toxins produced by the action of bacteria and viruses.

Mental or emotional, chemical and mechanical stress are the major categories of stress which we undergo every day. There are also other forms of stress that may have a negative impact on our lives, such as noise pollution and electromagnetic radiation.

A process of degeneration

Health

Stress factor 1,
e.g. mechanical
stress such as
a fall

No adaptation

Reduced efficiency
of function

Stress factor 2,
e.g. chemical
stress after
inhaling insecticide

No adaptation

Further reduction of
function

Stress factor 3,
e.g. emotional stress
such as shock

No adaptation

Body now
vulnerable to illness

Each time stress overload occurs, whatever the cause, the tension locks into the body, reducing its efficiency. Therefore it is less able to deal with any additional stress it may face, and a vicious circle develops. Each time it fails to adapt, more body stress is stored and the body enters a process of degeneration, with increased vulnerability to illness.

> Each time stress overload occurs … tension locks into the body, reducing its efficiency.

The American Medical Association has estimated that 80 per cent of disease can be ascribed to stress. In this statement, only mental stress is being considered. If we add mechanical and chemical stress to the equation, then the percentage would surely be higher.

A young man told us an amusing story of how he was attacked by all three categories of stress simultaneously. He was working feverishly at his computer during a work crisis and the department manager kept interrupting him – mental stress. Something went wrong with the computer, and he had to bend at an awkward angle to lift it out of the shelf to reach behind it – mechanical stress. A wire had broken free and while soldering it back in place he breathed in the soldering fumes – chemical stress. At that precise moment he remembered that he had forgotten a vital occasion, his girlfriend's birthday the previous day – instant emotional stress!

CHAPTER 7

What is body stress?

When stress overload occurs, the body immediately activates its resources to correct the situation.

For example, if you step off a pavement and twist your ankle, muscles may tighten around the joint and swelling will occur in order to immobilise the area. If you are wise and co-operate with your body, you rest the ankle and keep pressure off it, to allow the healing to take place. If your body succeeds in adapting to the force of the injury, after a few hours or days the swelling will go down, muscles relax to their normal tone, and full flexibility will return to the joint.

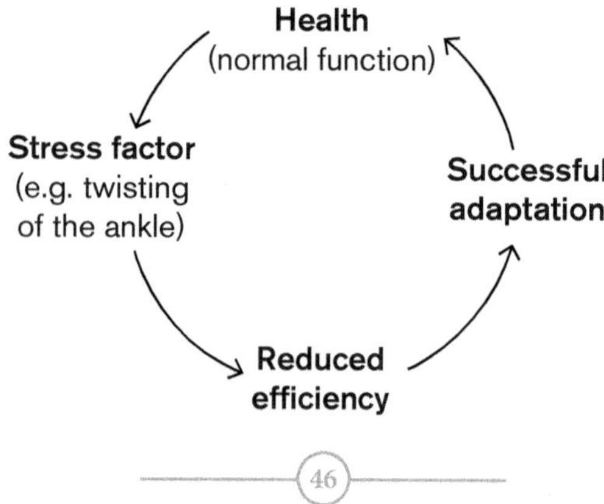

However, if the stress to the joint goes beyond the body's ability to adapt, some tension will remain held in the ankle. At times you may feel twinges of pain, or it may not regain its full range of motion. This is 'body stress', and it must be precisely detected and released for full function to be restored.

Body stress is a term that refers to any tension that is stored in a physical structure, which the body has not managed to release.

Sites of body stress are not visible on X-ray. They are accurately detected only by carrying out precise stress tests, using the body as a biofeedback mechanism. This means that the automatic responses of the body provide the necessary information.

Main sites of body stress

Stress may become locked into any part of the body, but it occurs most often around the spine. The main areas are the neck and the lower back – these are the most flexible sections and tend to become overloaded with mechanical stress – heavy lifting, twisting movements, sitting hunched, overexertion in exercise, etc.

A series of reactions occurs in stress overload. Imagine that you lift a heavy object while bending forward and twisting. The lower back takes the strain instead of the thigh muscles. If the muscles are challenged beyond their holding power, you will feel a jab of pain and the muscles of your lower back will lock into a spasm.

A frantic client once phoned about her husband. He had bent over the dog kennel to lift it, his lower back had 'locked up' and he dropped the kennel and collapsed on top of it. He was lying draped over its roof, unable to move. Fortunately we did not have to work on him in this position. After twenty minutes his wife was able to help him slide off the kennel, and by the time we arrived he had crawled into the house and onto the bed.

The muscle contractions may pull the spine into a forward arch, or tilt it sideways. With rest, the tension of the long back muscles may let go, but some tightness remains deep in the back. If you ignore the situation, you may start feeling pain radiating down a leg, or some numbness may occur in your toes. In addition you may begin to experience heartburn, or constipation, or a sensation of pressure in your bladder.

What has happened?

In straining the back, these things occur:

1. A compressive force is exerted on the openings between the vertebrae. This causes pressure around the spinal nerves that emerge from the spinal cord through these openings.
2. The short, deepest muscles which connect the vertebrae tighten at the vulnerable site, to immobilise it.
3. Then the longer, more superficial muscle groups contract in order to further limit movement. Thus, muscles which normally have the functions of support and movement have taken on a defensive role.
4. The increased muscle contraction exerts further pressure on the spinal nerves which emerge between the lumbar vertebrae. These nerves have pathways which supply the legs.

The compression may affect the sensory fibres in the nerves, and transmit an impulse throughout the length of the nerves, so pain or other sensations may be felt in the buttock, leg or foot. The motor nerve fibres may also be disturbed, leading to weakness of muscles supplied by the nerves under pressure. In addition, there are nerve connections with the internal organs, so there is disrupted communication, resulting in inefficiency or malfunction.

The mechanism of body stress

The moment the point of stress overload is reached, the body's survival response is triggered automatically by a reflex reaction. To illustrate this: if you accidentally touch a hot plate on the stove, your arm instantly jerks away. This immediate defensive reaction is caused by nerve connections in the spinal cord, independently of your brain and conscious awareness. This is called a reflex arc – the sensory signals from the pain receptors in the hand pass to the motor nerves in the cord, which activate the withdrawal reflex.

In the same way body stress locks instantly and automatically into physical structures, manifesting as a line of tension over a muscle, tendon, ligament, cartilage, or any body tissue.

Nerves are irritated at the stressed site, causing surrounding tissues to tighten in an effort to protect the area. The overlying muscles then contract in order to further restrict movement. The body takes these actions in order to make the best of a bad situation, to limit mobility and greater damage. However, with the muscles in this tightened, protective state, more pressure builds up around the nerves. In addition, tension exerted on a joint may lead to erratic movement, causing a clicking sensation.

How the situation may worsen

If the stored tension is not released it results in the body taking increased protective action, by progressively locking up more layers of back muscles. In this way further and more widespread sites become involved to compensate for the original area of body stress.

For example, a small site of body stress may arise in the upper back. In time the pain and stiffness may be felt throughout the neck, shoulder and middle back, as the large kite-shaped surface muscle tightens – it attaches to the back of the head and the shoulders and extends down to below the shoulder blades.

Further aggravation may arise when the tight muscles cause the discs between the vertebrae to become compressed. If they have been weakened by repeated abuse in the past, one may even bulge slightly and exert pressure on a spinal nerve. As each spinal nerve supplies a large area, there may be many distressing consequences of this pressure.

Why does the body not release the tension?

As the wisdom of the body is constantly overseeing all functions, why does it not correct the situation?

The brain's filtering mechanism

With its millions of cross-linked nerve connections, the brain simultaneously processes an immense amount of information. Messages are continuously transmitted to the brain from our sense organs, from special receptors in muscles which carry awareness about the position of our limbs, from chemical receptors in blood vessels, providing information about the level of substances in the blood, etc.

There is a group of nerves in the brain stem and mid-brain which form the reticular activating system, a mechanism which either passes nerve impulses on to the higher areas of the brain, or blocks them. In this way it acts as a screening device, suppressing certain information. This filtering effect is vital to our well-being. Our sensory organs are constantly registering an enormous amount of information – sights and sounds, and the sense of touch, such as the pressure of a chair or clothes on our skin, etc. Imagine if our brain was bombarded with all this information – if it reached our consciousness we would be overwhelmed.

The reticular activating system deals with the deluge of information by looking for patterns among the impulses arriving, and responding only when a certain number of more or less identical impulses are received.

In this way relevant messages are forwarded – that information which is new, or a threat, or which requires our awareness because some action needs to be taken. For example, when a repetitive sound occurs, such as the ticking of a clock, after a while we cease to be aware of it.

It appears that when a certain degree of nerve compression exists, there is a 'dampening down' effect on the nerves that connect the stressed area to the brain, so insufficient messages are relayed to the brain. Therefore when body stress is present, the brain's awareness of it is blocked, the body is not instructed to take action, and the tension remains stored.

It is the purpose of BSR to locate the exact sites of tension and provide the correct stimuli to the area, in such a way that the brain registers the presence of the body stress and becomes aware that action needs to be taken. It will then issue commands to the muscles to release the locked-in pressure, so that the muscles return to normal tone. Thus the body restores its natural state of balance and the normal flow of life energy, activating its inbuilt healing mechanisms.

'Patterns' of body stress

Tension does not become stored in the body simply at a point – body stress occurs as lines of tension. It becomes locked into the tissues in specific directions. So it is not a matter of dealing with so-called 'pressure points'.

Another important fact: body stress appears not at one site only, but as a complex of many sites. For example, in the lower back, the tension will occur over the whole lumbar area; in the neck it occurs over several

vertebrae, never just one. *In each area the body stress manifests as a 'pattern' of multiple lines of tension* – this shows that although body stress is a disorganising force, the body deals with the stored stress in a highly organised way.

In addition, the stressed areas are inter-connected. In BSR we have found that we cannot deal with the body in a fragmented way. If a person has pain in the neck, it is necessary to test for and release any stress that may be present in the whole spine. The neck will not stabilise unless the rest of the spine is stress-free.

The expensive three-month mystery

Celeste, aged thirteen, had a two-year history of headaches, nausea, vomiting and vision problems. For the past three months the intense headaches and migraines had been almost constant, and she was spending approximately as much time in bed as at school. She had been taken to a number of specialists, and was currently on a beta blocker and pain medication. The medical bills for the three months added up to a huge amount.

At her first BSR session, the practitioner pointed out to her mother that the muscles in Celeste's back were ridged and in spasm. The mother was sceptical, 'But that's her lower back. It's her headaches that are the problem.' The practitioner explained how tension in the lumbar spine has an impact on the whole spine and the cranium, via the long muscles that extend from the sacrum to the skull. Both mother and daughter were amazed at the possibility that, after all the treatments and medications which had been futile, someone could at last tell them exactly what the source of the problem was. They were even more incredulous when he began releasing the body stress, working very precisely and quite lightly.

On Celeste's second visit, three days later, there were hugs all round. Mother and daughter excitedly reported that she had experienced no migraines at all, and only one mild headache. By the third session, there had been no recurrence of pain. Three-and-a-half weeks later, at a follow-up session, Celeste said she felt 'brilliant'.

A person may have persistent pain between the shoulder blades, and undergo various forms of treatment to the area with little improvement. In such a case the BSR tests often reveal little body stress in the upper back, but a great deal of tension stored in the lower back. This causes the long back muscles to tighten and exert a pull on the shoulder blade region. Thus the site of discomfort may not be the source of the problem.

Postural compensation

The brain always strives to maintain a balanced position, in both the vertical and horizontal planes. This means that if tension locks into the spine, causing it to tilt to one side, the brain will direct muscles to exert a pull in the opposite direction, so that the head and brain remain upright.

If, for example, a sideways curve develops in the lower spine, a curve to the opposite side will occur higher up. In some cases the pelvis tilts up on one side, so that one leg appears to be shorter than the other. If a heel lift is placed in the shoe, this would be a matter of treating an effect, and may compound the problem.

Many people believe that, as we grow older, it is unavoidable that we lose our straight posture, and develop the postural distortions of old age. This is not true. At any age, if body stress becomes stored in the spine, a process of postural changes will be triggered. Once the body stress is released, the body will begin restoring the normal curves, as long as there is no disease causing the distortions.

At any age, if body stress becomes stored in the spine, the posture will begin to distort.

The process of distortion

Imagine a person with extremely poor posture. The lower back is rounded, the belly sagging, and the upper back is hunched, with slumped shoulders. There is contraction of the chest, and the neck is jutting forward, with the chin pulling downwards. Walking may be affected, with a tendency to sway from side to side like a penguin. How would a person in this state be feeling? The tightened muscles will cause stiffness of the whole spine, with restriction of movement in the neck and pelvis. There will very likely be pain in the lower back and neck, aching between the shoulder blades

and possibly headaches. The jaw may feel tense, and diaphragm tension may be inducing indigestion or heartburn.

This picture represents a spine with muscles in a constant state of contraction, as the body struggles to keep the head and brain level. If a young person has this kind of posture, he or she will probably be admonished to, 'Stand up straight! Don't slouch!' However, the poor posture is not the result of laziness – it is beyond conscious control.

As long as the body stress remains stored in the spine, the body will keep these compensatory mechanisms in play. In time, the contracted muscles may cause further sites of body stress, which in turn leads to greater muscle tension – a vicious circle.

If the body stress is released, these distortions can be reversed. Even in old age, the body is capable of restoring the natural curves to the spine, to an extent that is only limited by any structural degeneration that is present.

The impact of body stress on the nervous system

Body stress may occur anywhere in the body, causing lines of tension in structures like muscles, ligaments, tendons, cartilage, joints – in fact, in any tissue.

When tension becomes stored in a physical structure, the tissue is compressed, causing irritation of nerves. This results in either over-activity or under-activity of nerve transmission. The functioning of body parts or organs supplied by the nerves involved will be disturbed, for example body stress affecting the digestive system may lead to either diarrhoea or constipation.

Body stress in the spine has the most far-reaching effects, as each spinal nerve supplies a large area of the body, both on the surface and internally. When tension locks into other areas, for example a wrist, the disturbance of nerve impulses will be more localised and limited.

Body stress may be the hidden cause

When a health problem persists, in spite of a variety of treatments, one needs to consider whether the source of the condition has been overlooked. Dealing with effects will not resolve the situation if the cause is not addressed. If a light goes out, you can keep putting in new bulbs, and

if that does not work, you would surely go to the fuse box to find the origin of the fault.

Clients have often undergone many different treatments before trying BSR. When symptoms improve or clear up after stored tension has been located and released, it is a clear indication that the cause lay in a disruption of the communication system of the body.

Ewald's treatments

In Ewald's case, for thirty years the symptoms, or effects, of his problems were addressed, and not the causes.

> In his teens, his lower-back pain was assumed to be a kidney infection, and he was treated with penicillin. The source of the pain turned out to be body stress in the lumbar spine.
> When his knees began collapsing, he was advised to have exploratory surgery of the knees. Fortunately he did not go this route – the compression of the spinal nerves in the lower back was being referred to the knees.
> As he had difficulty breathing through the nose, a doctorrecommended an operation to widen the nasal passages. He resisted this drastic procedure, and later he found that the release of body stress in the neck restored communication to his respiratory system, and his nose no longer felt blocked.
> He had sinus problems and multiple allergies, e.g. to feathers and house dust, and was treated with a programme of desensitisation injections, with no effect. Again, once the tension in his neck was fully released, his body no longer reacted to these triggers.

Body stress is defined as: lines of tension stored in physical structures, as a result of stress overload, which disturb the normal tone of the body and undermine the efficiency of its communication system.

CHAPTER 8

Effects of body stress

The definition of body stress – lines of tension which are stored in physical structures – gives the impression of a minor, even innocuous situation. You may be thinking: how serious can a bit of tension be? Because of the impact on the nervous system, the effects of body stress range from mild to debilitating. Body stress may manifest as:

- pain
- numbness
- muscle weakness
- stiffness, with restricted movement and loss of flexibility
- distorted posture
- joint degeneration
- tiredness
- psychological effects
- disturbed function

Pain

The most common reason people come for BSR is to seek relief from pain, mainly in the lower back, neck and shoulder area, and headaches. Of course we all want to be free of pain. Instead of covering it up with drugs, or suppressing it in some other way, we need to deal with the cause. As body stress causes compression of nerves, it usually results in pain. However, the presence of pain may have a variety of meanings.

The significance of pain

- Pain serves as a warning system, alerting us that some degenerative process, tissue damage or disease is present, or that there is pressure on nerves, interfering with the body's communication system.
- When a painful stimulus irritates a nerve receptor, if the electrical charge generated builds up to firing point of the nerve, pain will be felt. If the pain is constant, it means that the level of irritation is above the firing point. If the locked-in stress is released, initially there may be little or no reduction of pain.
- The pain withdraws once the electrical charge drops below the firing point, and recurs if the person does some action which irritates the nerve back up to the threshold level. This is why pain comes and goes during a healing process, depending on how we use the body. The pain fluctuations after BSR are a positive sign that healing is taking place. A person needs to be patient and remember that healing is a process, and to listen to the body's signals, easing up on activities which re-stress the body.
- Pain may signify the start of the healing process, as pressure is removed from numbed nerves and sensation is restored – 'no feeling, no healing'.
- Pain may be 'masked', i.e. temporarily numbed. For example, a person may do vigorous exercise and find that their back pain disappears. However, the cause, which may be compression of nerves, is still present, and the pain returns when the person stops the exercise.
- Pain is often worst on waking. During the night of rest, muscles relax and the body withdraws from its defensive, protective state, so sensation is restored to the stressed areas. This is why people often get up and walk around to get some relief – as explained above, the re-tightening of the muscles reinstates the numbing effect.

- Pain often builds up later in the day. This is because the day's activities have overridden the holding capacity of the deeply locked muscles, forcefully reinstating mobility into the stressed area the body was protecting. As the irritation level in the nerves rises, the superficial muscles tighten to again restrict movement, adding stiffness to the pain.
- Pain may move into a different area during the healing process. For example, compression in the lower back may cause the spinal nerves affected to fire along the entire pathways down the leg, so pain registers right into the foot. After the pressure in the back is released, the pain may be felt in the calf, then in the thigh, then in the buttock, as the irritation to the nerves withdraws.
- Pain may not occur immediately after body stress locks into an area, and may be felt only days, weeks or months later. This is the result of an initial numbing effect, which wears off over time as the body seeks to regain its normal mobility.
- After body stress is released, pain may suddenly be experienced again, even when the individual has not re-stressed an area. This occurs when deeper muscles at the original compression site begin to relax. This means the body stress can now be released at a deeper level.

Other indications of body stress

Numbness

When stress has been locked into the body over a period of time, the area may cease to feel painful. Did you ever strain your lower back, and it ached at first, but after a while the pain disappeared? So you assumed it was fine. This is because the compression of the spinal nerves reduced sensation in the area. However, the areas served by those nerves will be affected, and one of the results could be patches of numbness. Pressure in the lower back may lead to numbness of toes or the sole of the foot. Body stress in the neck may cause numbness or tingling in the hands.

Muscle weakness

This is frequently experienced in the arms and hands, as well as in the spine in general. A woman in her sixties found that she had no strength in her hands when she woke up. After being up for about an hour she felt her hands had sufficient grip to hold a teacup. The BSR tests located

body stress in her lower neck, which is the area from which the spinal nerves emerge to supply the hands. The pressure in this area had been worsened by lying all night. After the tension was released, she could once again enjoy having her first cup of tea, sitting up in bed.

Stiffness

A farmer of fifty-seven complained of a very painful neck, with severely restricted movement. His head remained tilted to one side. His neck had bothered him on and off for about thirty years and he had tried many types of conventional and 'alternative' approaches, but nothing provided lasting relief. He also reported a lower-back injury that had occurred fourteen years before. As he did contract sheep-shearing he often spent days on end bent over.

His present bout of neck pain had lasted ten weeks. His physiotherapist had told him that his back was so tense and hard that she could 'do her ironing on it'. The BSR practitioner agreed with this description as he had to work on raised bands of muscles on either side of the spine when he carried out the stress releases in the lower back and neck. At the second session the farmer was beaming and declared himself 90 per cent better. The muscles throughout the back already felt more relaxed to the touch, even though the process of unlocking the tension was not yet complete.

Distorted posture

A woman in her seventies had osteoarthritis of the spine, and this degenerative condition had led to an extremely hunched posture – her whole back was bowed, with total loss of the lower-back curve. After three BSR sessions some of this natural curve was restored, and her upper back was less arched. This shows that only part of the distortion was due to her spinal degeneration; the rest was a result of tension stored in muscles. Even though she was still bowed over, she was very happy, as the reduction in muscle tension made her feel more upright, and she could now raise her head sufficiently to look at the faces of people as she spoke to them.

A postural distortion may come on suddenly, when a movement causes intense irritation to spinal nerves. A woman in her fifties was watering her garden with a hose when her back went into a spasm. That night the pain kept her from sleeping and the next day she had to use two sticks to walk, very slowly, bent over to one side. The day after the lower-back stress

releases she could walk with one stick, and after three sessions her spine was upright again. She felt some pain only if she sat in an awkward position. As it was a minor twisting movement that led to such intense compression of spinal nerves, it may be assumed that this woman had some tension stored deep in her lower back over a period of time.

After lifting a heavy object, a glamorous and attractive woman of forty arrived at the BSR practice bent almost double. She had to walk sideways like a crab and cling to the wall to make her way up the passage to the consulting room. She would have been mortified to hear the sympathetic comment of a young man in the reception area, 'That poor old lady! I wonder what's wrong with her?' Unfortunately he was not present when the same woman left, once again looking straight and youthful.

Joint degeneration

While pressure remains stored in a joint, the joint starts undergoing changes. Calcium is deposited around the joint in the body's attempt to give support to an unstable area. The edges of the bones become roughened, and bony outgrowths, called osteophytes, start developing. Compare this with an old building – if a wall starts to weaken and lean, a supporting wall may be built at an angle to shore it up. Over time the joint cartilage is affected and the joint shape distorts, causing pain and limited mobility. In this way it is possible that if body stress is not released, in time it may contribute to the development of osteoarthritis.

Tiredness

A person with body stress may feel tense or tired, lacking energy and zest for life. Tiredness is caused by energy being diverted into keeping muscles in a constant protective state. However, it is also possible for body stress to be present without the person being aware of any physical effects.

One businessman said he always knew when it was time to come for a BSR session as his thinking was becoming 'cloudy'.

Psychological effects

When tension is stored in the body, it has a psychologically draining effect, even in the absence of pain or other symptoms. A person may feel a sense of unease and anxiety, without being able to pinpoint the reason. The challenges of daily life may seem overwhelming, and there may be a tendency to withdraw, like a snail retreating into the safety of its shell.

Afraid of life

Marina was referred to BSR by a friend, but it took all her courage to actually make an appointment. She phoned three times, and on the third call she decided that she liked the practitioner's voice, and she would take the risk of going. It was a frightening challenge for Marina, as she had developed a terror of leaving her home and could not even contemplate driving a car. At sixty-four, a retired dance teacher, she had withdrawn into a lonely sanctuary of depression and extreme anxiety, and turned her back on the world. She also had vertigo and ringing in the ears.

Her husband scoffed at the idea that BSR could help her, and said it would be a waste of money.

The practitioner released tension in her neck and lower back, and over her solar plexus. After the first session the vertigo was only slight, and she felt generally better. After the second, her husband offered to pay for her to go to BSR daily, if necessary, as the changes in her were so remarkable. A week later, after the third session, it was as though an oppressive, constricting force was removed from her body and mind. Not only was she no longer afraid to go out, she started driving again. She joined a dance group and said she was beginning to enjoy life once more. Some months later she had a few more BSR sessions, for relief of upper- and lower-back pain.

'Soul tension'

Ariana, a very tall, slim student of twenty-four, had no physical problems. But her whole life, as far back as she could remember, she had been aware that her body was holding extreme tension. Her first BSR session brought on a flood of sensations – pain all along her right side, stomach ache and lower-back stiffness. After another session her neck began hurting, and she experienced strange movements and wind in her digestive system.

At the fourth appointment, the young woman looked transformed – her expression was bright and happy. She told the practitioner that on the morning after the third session she had a profound experience. The moment she woke up she felt twenty-four years of tension surge to the surface, and she burst into tears. She cried for half an hour 'from the depth of her soul'.

Ariana said she felt a heavy but undefined burden had been taken off her shoulders. She was relaxed and more at ease with herself, and sleeping better than she had ever done.

Disturbed function

Because body stress exerts pressure on nerves, it leads to a disturbance of the body's communication system. So it could be described as a disruption to the normal life energy flow in the body.

We are usually aware of its effects on more superficial areas of our body, such as pain, stiffness, etc. in our back or limbs. But it also has an impact on the nerve supply to internal structures, thus there is a decline in the efficiency of the body's ability to heal and maintain itself. In addition, the compression of tissue may affect blood vessels, and therefore circulation, and lymph vessels, disturbing the body's fluid drainage and filtration system.

Each new day brings another load of pressure – mechanical, chemical and emotional stresses. In its undermined state the body is less able to deal with these, so additional tension becomes stored. This further reduces the body's capacity to adapt to the stresses of living. Thus the life expression enters a continuous downward spiral of degeneration, with the individual moving increasingly further away from health. As the process goes on, a person may have forgotten the original cause of the stress overload, such as a fall or car accident. The individual comes to accept as normal any sense of having less than 100 per cent well-being, and may say, 'It's my age', or, 'Cold weather always makes my joints ache', or, 'It's to be expected – my mother also had numb feet.'

People try to deal with stress overload with excessive drinking, overeating, using drugs, overexercising, etc. – and end up introducing more stress into their lives.

CHAPTER 9

Body stress in specific areas

Lines of tension may become locked into any structure, anywhere in the body. However, compression of the spinal nerves potentially has a widespread effect, as the nerve connections supply a large body area and internal organs. By contrast, the impact of body stress in, for example, the wrist or knee will be more localised.

Viewed from the side, the spine has natural curves that give it strength and stability: a forward curve in the neck and lower back, and a backward curve in the chest region. The bodies of the vertebrae are bound together by the inter-vertebral discs, which allow flexibility and act as shock absorbers. (See Figure 2.)

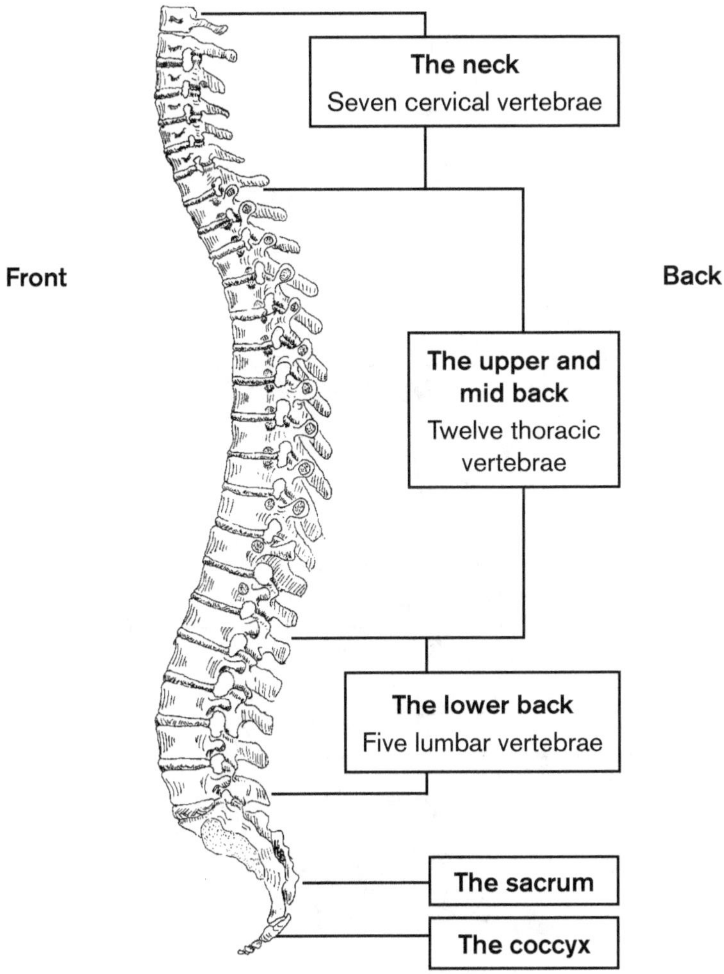

Figure 2: Side view of the spine

The lower back

In the lower back the spine has five lumbar vertebrae located above the sacrum, a triangular-shaped bone which fits between the bones of the pelvis with a sacroiliac joint on each side. The coccyx is a small tail-like bone below the sacrum.

The lumbar spine has a forward curve as the discs are wedge-shaped, thinner at the back and thicker at the front. (See Figure 3.)

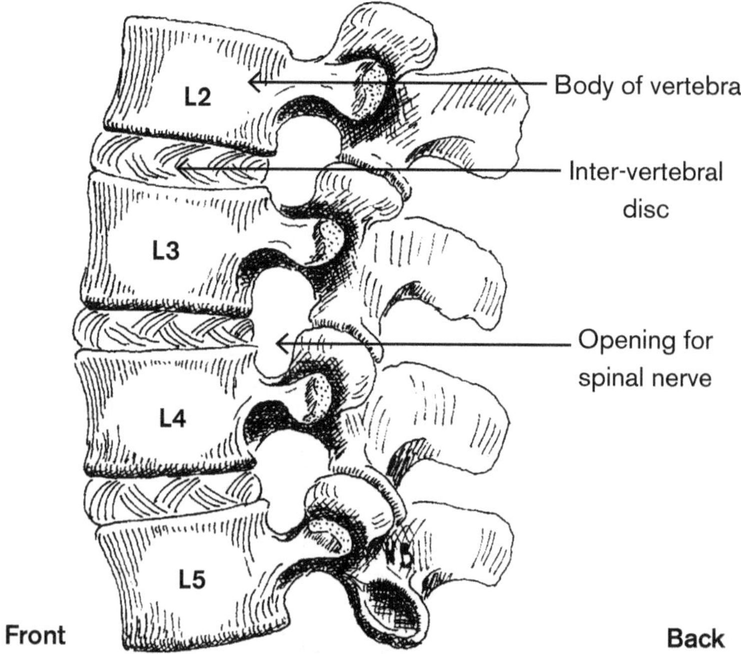

Figure 3: Side view of the lumbar spine (Vertebrae L2–L5) showing the forward curve of the lower back

The ring of bone behind the vertebral bodies forms a bony canal which contains the spinal cord. The spinal nerves emerge from the cord through openings between the vertebrae, and supply the skin and muscles of the legs and feet, the lower abdomen and groin areas. Branches from these nerves also lead to the internal organs, such as those of the digestive, reproductive and urinary systems.

Body stress in the lower back irritates the spinal nerves and may result in back pain, at times referred along the nerve pathways into the abdomen, groin, hips, legs or feet. Often pain is felt along the large sciatic nerve which passes through the buttock and down the back of the leg. People describe a wide range of sensations, such as, 'It feels like there are pebbles in my shoes,' and, 'Boiling water is being poured down the marrow of the bone.' Numbness in any of these areas may be experienced, also stiffness and muscle weakness. The compression effect in the lower back may be so severe that muscles lock up in a protective spasm, pulling the spine forwards or sideways.

Even when there is no pain, the presence of body stress in the lumbar spine causes a sense of unease. If you see a child who cannot sit still, or a person standing in a queue who is shuffling the feet, you can suspect they have lower-back stress, which keeps them moving in an attempt to ease the nerve pressure.

Living on painkillers

Karl, an electrical engineer of thirty-nine, described the pain in his legs as excruciating, and he could not sleep without taking pain medication. At times he tried to drive the pain away by pummelling his thighs so hard it created bruises. He was examined by neurologists, who concluded that his sciatic nerves were inflamed, but there was no apparent cause, and he would have to rely on painkillers 'until the pain went away'. His only other complaint was heartburn. The BSR stress tests revealed tension locked into the lower back, which was exerting a pull on the diaphragm muscle, and pressure over the coccyx. Immediately after the releases the leg pain lessened, and the lower

back started aching, showing that compression was being lifted from the area that was the source of the problem. After the second session he had no pain at all in the legs, and the lower back was improving. He could now sleep through the night and no longer needed painkillers. As a bonus, with the diaphragm free of tension, there was no more heartburn.

Some people are aware of tension building up in the lower back, and may ignore it for years. As layers of muscles tighten over time, a person may feel the back growing stiffer and blame it on ageing. Then one day a slight movement, like a twist or stretch, may cause the lower back to go instantly into a painful spasm. This extra stress has finally overridden the holding ability of the protectively tightened deep muscles and triggered the surface muscles into locking up in order to restrict movement.

Causes of body stress in the lower back

The jarring effect of *accidents and falls* may cause body stress to become stored in the lower back. Also, *heavy or incorrect lifting or bending* may strain ligaments and muscles, and compress the discs. The *wrong kinds of exercise* – those involving twisting movements or repeated forward bending – may stress the lumbar spine. Another cause is *poor posture*, especially sitting in a slumped position, which reverses the normal lumbar curve.

Sitting like this may give temporary relief from back pain, as it causes the joint spaces to open up at the back and thus reduces pressure on spinal nerves for a short time. However, this posture builds up compression of the discs and in time the back walls of the discs may weaken and start bulging. This could result in greater pressure being exerted on a spinal nerve. Over time the bulge may increase and develop into a herniation (prolapse) of the disc, in which the pulpy centre pushes into the protruding fibrous outer part, resulting in intense nerve irritation. (See Figure 4.)

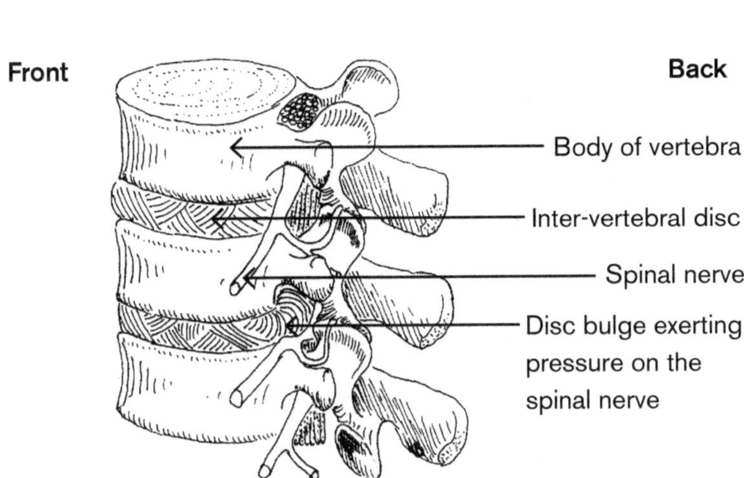

Figure 4: Side view of three vertebrae showing a normal disc and a bulging disc

Calf pain

A man of forty-eight was experiencing such severe calf pain that he was unable to walk. He arrived at our practice suspended between his wife and son, hanging onto their shoulders. He told us that he had just completed a week of traction in hospital, but it had not eased his pain. He was not aware of any pain in his lower back, but the BSR checks indicated the presence of body stress in that area. After the first set of releases he felt a surge of pain in his lower back, as feeling was restored to numbed nerves. The calf pain was unchanged. After the second session three days later, the pain withdrew from the calves. He was now experiencing deep pain in his hips and thighs, and the lower-back pain remained intense. Following the third session five days later he reported a lessening of the lower-back pain. Within two weeks he was pain-free and was able to return to work. This case illustrates the fact that the sites of pain may be referred from body stress in the spine. The area of origin was numb initially, and only once communication was restored could the healing process be activated. In cases like this the saying 'no feeling, no healing' applies.

Foot rotation

A thirty-one-year-old woman had walked with one foot rotated outwards ever since a motor accident in her teens. She frequently woke with her lower back in extreme pain, and had to be lifted out of bed. She underwent regular BSR over a three-month period. Gradually her foot returned to normal position, and her buttock muscles, which had been wasted, rebuilt.

Another woman in her forties had experienced lower-back pain most of her life. She mentioned that she had always walked with both feet turned outwards, 'like a clown', according to her husband. After several BSR sessions, one morning she fell forward as she got out of bed and tried to walk. Both feet had rotated back and were now pointing straight forward. Her children supported her while she walked up and down the passage, until it felt normal to be walking with straight feet.

Effects on internal organs

An often quoted statistic is that lower-back pain will affect 80 per cent of adults at some stage of their life. However, most people are unaware that pain is only one of the effects of tension locked into the lumbar spine. While body stress remains stored in the lower back, the pressure on the nerves may undermine or disturb the normal functioning of the areas and organs they supply. Thus body stress may lead to digestive problems, such as constipation or diarrhoea, bladder complaints, sexual problems, etc. A very common complaint is severe menstrual cramps and pain, which often cease when the lower-back compression is released.

Incontinence

A woman in her late seventies described herself as very active, and said that she did not have any back problems needing attention. She decided to experience BSR out of interest in 'healthy methods'. The practitioner released tension in her neck and lower back, and gave her advice about posture. After several visits the client asked whether BSR could help other areas of the body, not just the back. She went on to explain that she had been too embarrassed to mention that she had been suffering from incontinence, but it was now at an end, and she was so relieved to no longer have to wear 'those awful adult nappies'.

Constipation and foot pain

These two seemingly unrelated problems came from the same source in a woman in her thirties. She had undergone surgery for pain in one foot. There was no improvement, and she came for BSR as the other foot had started to ache as well. Body stress was focused in her lower spine – the area that supplies nerves to both the legs and the digestive system. Her husband phoned later to say it had taken them a long time to drive home. His wife had started having copious diarrhoea, and they had been obliged to stop at the toilet of every filling station on their way back. When he explained that she had been having a problem with constipation for years, it became clear that the body had taken advantage of the restoration of communication to the bowels to deal with the condition without delay.

Infertility

A woman in her mid-twenties was longing for a baby, but her gynaecologist found that she was not ovulating. Also, her knee and foot reflexes were absent, which implied some spinal nerve compression. She came to BSR because of long-term lower-back pain. After several months of regular releases her back had improved and she became pregnant. She received another bonus – it turned out to be twins.

Lower-back pain brought a woman in her thirties to BSR. She had two daughters, the youngest being eight. She and her husband had assumed their family was complete, as she had not fallen pregnant in the years after the second child. A few months later she was shocked to find she was pregnant. Their initial dismay turned to joy, as she gave birth to the son they thought they would never have.

Another couple who had been married for eighteen years had long resigned themselves to being childless. The wife had undergone several operations for endometriosis, and was considered sterile. After about a year of regular BSR she fell pregnant, and in awe and excitement they started planning for a whole new future.

Bladder infections

A young woman suffered from recurrent bouts of bladder infection. The problem would clear after a course of antibiotics, but soon recur along with lower-back stiffness. After three sessions of BSR the cystitis ceased. With many women who are prone to this problem, we have checked them just as they were feeling the first threatening signs of bladder irritation. After the releases it did not progress to an infection – the nerve communication was restored, the immune system was boosted back to efficiency, and was able to deal with the problem.

Reduced sexual function

As the nerves in the lower back connect to the sex organs, compression in this area may undermine sexual function. A man in his forties hoped that BSR would reduce his lower-back and leg pain, but he received an additional benefit. On his second visit he confided to his practitioner that his libido was restored. He had been too embarrassed to mention his sexual problem to her, and had not realised that it could be related to his back. 'My wife is very happy,' he smiled.

By contrast, a man of seventy-five was astounded at the return of his sexual desire and function, and somewhat dismayed. 'My wife isn't pleased at all – she says I'm really annoying her.'

A woman in her late forties found that intercourse was no longer painful after the body stress in the lower back and pelvic area was released.

The mid and upper back

There are twelve thoracic (chest area) vertebrae, creating a natural backward curve, with twelve pairs of ribs forming the ribcage which contains the heart and lungs. At the front of the body the upper ten ribs are attached to the sternum (breastbone) by means of cartilage. Below the ribs, the large diaphragm muscle has attachments to the sternum, the lower ribs and the vertebrae of the lower spine. On the back, the flat shoulder-blade bones are positioned over the ribs. The spinal nerves emerge from the spinal cord through openings between the vertebrae, and supply the skin and muscles of the back and chest. They also have branches going internally to the heart and respiratory system.

The effect of body stress may be a mild nagging ache in the upper back

between the shoulder blades, or a persistent itching. It may also manifest as a severe stabbing pain between the ribs, which is worsened by deep breathing, as this increases the pull on the muscles between the ribs.

Causes of body stress in the mid and upper back

The chest and back areas may be strained by working in a hunched or twisted posture, e.g. bending over a sewing machine, doing woodwork, etc. Body stress may be caused by lifting heavy objects and/or holding them up for a long time.

Body stress may also occur as a painful spasm of the diaphragm muscle. The diaphragm forms a 'floor' between the chest and the abdominal cavities, and plays a major role in breathing. As it contracts, air is pulled into the lungs, and when it relaxes air is pushed out. Besides the mechanical factors mentioned above, the cause may be emotional tension, such as anxiety, the 'butterflies in the stomach' feeling. Or the diaphragm may tighten as a result of irritation from eating or drinking something spicy, acid or very cold.

Another cause of diaphragm stress is bloating – gas is produced in certain people who have difficulty digesting foods like wheat, or when eating sugary foods, or combinations of foods, like orange juice with cereal.

A pseudo heart attack

After cutting his lawn with a heavy mower, Don, a man in his forties, gulped down a glass of iced orange juice. Suddenly he experienced severe chest pain and breathlessness. A cardiologist conducted several tests, and assured him that there was nothing wrong with his heart. Don was convinced the specialist had missed something, as the condition persisted for weeks. His anxiety level soared as daily he woke up wondering if today would bring on his looming heart attack. Finally he came for BSR hoping for some relief. The tests for body stress indicated tension over the sternum, ribs and diaphragm, as well as in the spine. After the releases all pain withdrew and did not recur. Not only was he relieved of his sense of foreboding, but his faith in the medical profession was restored.

Stomach pain

A woman of thirty enjoyed going on 'fun runs', but after each race she had such intense abdominal pain that she thought she would have to give up running. In her BSR assessment, the stressed areas included the diaphragm and chest. On being questioned she realised that she had the habit of downing a cold, fizzy drink after each race. After that she switched to drinking water, and continued to run races without any stomach pain.

Constant hunger

Tension in the diaphragm exerts a pull on the oesophagus, which passes through it. This resembles the movement of food making its way to the stomach and sends a signal to the stomach to concentrate the hydrochloric acid to break down the anticipated food. The effect is a burning, gnawing sensation. Many people experience this sense of always being hungry, and they eat all day long to relieve the acidity, which of course leads to weight gain. After releasing the diaphragm and related areas of body stress the 'hunger pains' cease, and weight loss follows.

The bayonet in the back

An artist of sixty-eight described his pain as 'a bayonet stuck in my back'. He also had breathlessness and pain into his shoulders and down one arm, and he experienced indigestion even if he had eaten only a biscuit. Painkillers did not help, and he felt he would rather be dead than have to endure the pain any longer. Immediately after the body stress was released the pain was gone. However, when he returned two days later, all the pain was back. He said he had felt so good after his first session that he had done some painting the next day. Once again after release the bayonet pain disappeared. He followed the practitioner's advice to work in an upright posture, rather than bending over the painting, and the pain did not return.

Pain in the breastbone

An engineer aged thirty-two was diagnosed with Guillain-Barré syndrome (a disease of the peripheral nerves), and had constant pain in the chest, with muscle cramps over the breastbone at night. The whole of his middle and upper back was rigid and very sensitive. As the BSR practitioner released the tension on the breastbone, he exclaimed, 'Unbelievable! The pain is gone.' It returned three days later, but less intense. Again, as the area was released, he said, 'It's gone, it's gone!' The pain went through a process of coming and going, and ceased entirely after five sessions.

Continuous belching

It sounds humorous, the idea of someone belching all the time. But the reality for Freda, a housewife in her fifties, was far from funny. The burps were extremely loud, one following directly after the other. What brought this on? It is significant that the past few years had been extremely stressful for Freda, as she had lost seven members of her family. She was holding tension in her neck and diaphragm, and had cramping of the fingers and heartburn, as well as depression.

Body stress was released in the neck, back and diaphragm. At first there was no relief from the belching, although her other problems improved. Over the next four sessions the burping steadily reduced in frequency, then stopped altogether.

Hiatus hernia

Is the diaphragm connected to the nose? A woman of sixty had a gastroscopy and was diagnosed with a hiatus hernia. In this condition the upper part of the stomach pushes up into the chest cavity, through

the oesophageal opening in the diaphragm. She was experiencing acid reflux, heartburn and breathlessness, as well as headaches, tight fingers on waking, and back and leg pain.

All the symptoms eased after BSR, and she noticed something else. She asked the practitioner, 'Could what you did have affected my nose?' She had always had a weak sense of smell, and now for the first time she could smell the sea. Other odours were much more powerful, so much so that she had to hold strong-smelling foods at arm's length.

The logical connection in this case is the neck. The lower neck supplies nerves to the diaphragm, as well as to the arms and hands, and also connects to nerves of the lining of the nose.

The neck

There are seven cervical (neck) vertebrae, forming a natural forward curve. As in the rest of the spine, the vertebral bodies are joined by the inter-vertebral discs, which act as shock absorbers. The spinal nerves supply the skin and muscles of the shoulders, arms and hands.

Body stress stored in the neck structures may cause pain and stiffness, and an inability to turn the head fully. Tension referred from the neck may affect nerves and blood vessels and result in headaches or pain in the face or jaw. There may be sensations of dizziness or nausea.

As the nerves to the arms originate in the lower neck, pain or numbness may occur in the shoulder, arm or hand. Muscles may be weakened, resulting in difficulty in grasping objects.

These effects are quite straightforward to understand because of the layout of the nerves in the neck. But can body stress of the neck have even more dramatic or profound effects on the body? Could it affect the senses of sight, hearing, smell and taste?

In the neck there are connections to nerve pathways of the autonomic nervous system, which lead to the eyes, ears, nose and mouth, as well as to the internal organs of the chest and abdomen.

Neck stress may disturb the normal functioning of the senses, and cause other effects, such as difficulty in swallowing, a burning, dry mouth, or excess saliva. It may also undermine the efficiency of the heart, lungs and digestive system. This explains why releasing pressure in the neck

may result in so-called miracles. (Miracles are natural occurrences which are merely unexpected.)

There is another reason why neck tension may have such a far-reaching negative effect on the body as a whole: every spinal nerve arises from nerve tracts which must first pass through the cervical area of the spinal cord.

Ear pain of unknown origin

A student of nineteen had ear pain for nine months. An ENT specialist could find no cause, and prescribed pain medication. The BSR practitioner released body stress in the neck and lower back. After the first session the neck felt more mobile, and the ear pain withdrew entirely after the second session.

Tinnitus

The day after body stress was released in his neck, a man noticed that the sound of the ringing in his ears had changed in tone. The following day the noise ceased. This shows that in this case the cause of the tinnitus lay in the cervical nerve connections to the ear, and was not caused by any defect in the hearing apparatus itself.

Causes of body stress in the neck

Mechanical causes include jarring or jerking the neck in a fall or a whiplash in a car accident; working or reading with the head tilted downwards for lengthy periods; and twisting the neck as when reversing a car. Remember Halley's comet? For several nights everyone was straining to see this once-in-a-lifetime phenomenon, head tilted back to scan the sky. In our practice we had several cases of 'comet neck'.

Emotional stresses like anger, anxiety and shock cause a person to hunch the shoulders and tighten the neck muscles. Exposure to harmful chemicals may severely irritate the nervous system and result in tension in the neck muscles.

An old neck injury

An array of health problems may be traced back to a past trauma of the neck. A woman in her forties started having multiple symptoms – increasing dizziness, sharp pains that moved from knee to wrist to elbow, hand and foot numbness, and frequent migraine headaches. Her head felt so heavy that she could no longer read. This continued for six years and exhaustion and despair plunged her into a deep depression. She had a series of BSR sessions over several months, and gradually the symptoms cleared. The original cause? She remembered a car accident twelve years before. Tension had locked into her neck in that whiplash, but it took six years for the impact on the nervous system to build up to the point of severely disturbing function.

Effects on the arms

For four years Tina, aged fifty, had a stiff neck and daily headaches, and she accepted these as her lot in life. Her real problem, she said, was her left elbow. It was so painful she could not sleep on her left side, and she was unable to lift the arm at all. She had been to numerous doctors and other practitioners, to no avail, and now lived on painkillers. Her arm had been X-rayed, and appeared normal. No X-rays had been taken of the neck, although this proved to be the source of the arm problem. As tension was released from her neck Tina felt immediate relief, and could raise her arm slightly. By her third BSR session her arm was functioning normally and was pain-free, and she had no more headaches.

Neck immobility

A man in his early twenties had been diagnosed with neuralgia of the neck. He had intense, constant pain on both sides, with little movement. He also felt unrelenting pins and needles in his arms, and lower-back stiffness. He realised that his problems dated back to a car accident seven years before, as well as several concussions he had suffered playing rugby.

A variety of medical and alternative treatments had not helped, and he felt despondent as he could no longer do any form of sport or exercise. Body stress was released throughout his spine, as well as his chest. Initially his neck pain increased and he had several headaches, although the arm sensations diminished. The next three sessions were a roller-coaster ride of ups and downs, as the neck pain and rigidity lessened then worsened. This takes place as the body progressively unlocks layers of tension, and sensation is restored to compressed nerves. By the fifth appointment the young man struggled to hold back tears of relief when he showed the practitioner that he could turn his head fully from side to side. He was amazed the process had taken only two weeks.

Improved vision

A man in his fifties had been wearing glasses for decades. After several sessions of BSR he was startled to find they were distorting his vision, so he removed them. His wife was dismayed, 'I'm not going in the car with you if you're driving without your glasses.' He assured her repeatedly that he could see perfectly well without them. During the argument she plonked herself down on the couch, and happened to land on his glasses, breaking them. That ended the debate, and he

demonstrated his safe driving without them. However, she was only convinced when he visited his optometrist, and the tests proved her husband's vision to be normal.

Another man in his sixties found that during the year after he had six sessions of BSR, his vision gradually improved to the point where he could dispense with his thick, bifocal spectacles, even though he had no further releases.

Asthma

A woman in her thirties experienced a sudden onset of breathing difficulties, and was diagnosed as having asthma. After four months her condition had not improved in spite of medication, and she was referred to a psychiatrist, to address any emotional factors that might be contributing to the problem. At that stage she came for BSR because of a stiff neck.

In the case history she mentioned that she had suffered a whiplash in a car accident four months before, but it had not occurred to her that this could relate to her asthma. However, there is a direct connection between neck stress and breathing, as the phrenic nerve, which supplies the diaphragm, originates from the third, fourth and fifth spinal nerves in the neck. After the body stress in the neck was released she estimated there was an 80 per cent improvement in her condition, and after the second appointment she declared herself 'cured'.

Allergies

Long-term asthma is often accompanied by allergic reactions.

Zara had a hypersensitivity to horses, manifesting as an allergic reaction and asthma attacks, therefore this all-round action woman in her mid-twenties did not include riding in her activities. As a champion

surfer she loved adventure sports, such as bunjee jumping. These took a toll on her cervical spine, which started improving with BSR.

When a friend asked her to take care of her horse for a few days, Zara was careful not to touch the animal. But just being close to the horse while putting out its food and water was enough to trigger her allergy – her eyes became red and swollen. Over the next few months, as the deep-seated compression was released from her neck, Zara ceased having asthma attacks. Once again she was asked to look after her friend's horse, and she was delighted to find that she had no adverse reactions at all.

A man in his thirties had a pollen allergy, and each spring brought on the wheezing, eye-streaming misery of hay fever. After three BSR sessions for neck stiffness, he was no longer affected by flowering plants or trees. Although he had no further sessions, his wife, a maintenance client, reported that the hay fever never returned. She was amused to observe that each spring he challenged the pollen by pushing his face into a particular former enemy flower, and inhaling deeply, but there was no sneezing and wheezing reaction.

Loss of voice

In BSR practices there have been several cases of people who had partially or entirely lost their voice. After the release of neck stress the voice was restored or improved. Each client had noticed that the problem was worse when they were tense. This makes sense, as the tightening of the neck muscles would add to the pressure on the nerve connections to the larynx, the voice box.

The head and face

BSR practitioners are able to test for body stress over the bones of the skull and the face, which may be caused by hitting the head. The tension in these areas may also be referred from body stress in the neck muscles which attach to the bones of the head and face. There may be compression of the cranial nerves, which arise in the brain and pass out of openings in the skull, leading to the face.

Trigeminal neuralgia (tic douloureux)

The trigeminal nerves are one of the twelve pairs of cranial nerves. On each side of the head, a trigeminal nerve has branches which carry sensation from the upper and middle areas of the face and from the jaw. When the nerve comes under pressure it may cause intense stabbing pain to radiate along its pathways, especially in the cheek, lips, chin and tongue. In a woman of fifty, it was so severe that she could barely eat, and spoke through gritted teeth. Even washing her face and slight tightening of the muscles caused the pain level to soar. As she walked, the movement of air over her face escalated the pain, so she kept the area covered with a cloth. Besides neck stress, the BSR tests pinpointed lines of tension at various sites on her skull and face. After the releases the hypersensitivity of the skin diminished, and the pain withdrew over the next several hours. She returned for BSR when the neuralgia recurred six months later, at a time when she was undergoing work pressure and emotional stress. She realised she had reacted to the stress by tightening her neck muscles. She determined to become more conscious of her response to stressful situations, and to wilfully relax the muscles of her upper back when starting to feel tense.

Bell's palsy

This is a paralysis, usually temporary, of the muscles on one side of the face, due to compression of a branch of the facial nerve (a cranial nerve). It had been present for two months in a fifty-year-old man. His sagging face and drooping eyelid caused him acute embarrassment and made him reluctant to meet people. The BSR session included the release of stress over the facial bones. Over the next few days the distortion of his facial features gradually disappeared.

The jaw

Biting into something hard or a blow to the jaw may directly induce body stress at one or both jaw joints (temporo-mandibular joint or TMJ), resulting in pain, restricted movement or clicking. Or, tension locked into other areas of the body may gradually lead to imbalance of neck muscles which attach to the jaw.

A domino effect

For Vanessa, it all started at seventeen, when she tore the anterior cruciate ligament in her knee in a hockey game. After surgery and months of rehabilitation, her difficulty in walking caused instability in her lower back. A few years later her work as a radiographer involved lifting patients and moving heavy equipment, and she developed lower-back pain. After a fall on her coccyx her life became a cycle of bladder and kidney infections, with a new course of antibiotics every few weeks. Pain migrated from her knee to her hip, and she was diagnosed with iliotibial-band friction syndrome.

When she was twenty-three Vanessa's jaw locked and she could barely open her mouth. Eating was difficult, when she spoke her mouth moved only slightly, and the pain was constant. She underwent a series of treatments with no improvement. At night she wore a bite plate to prevent her from clenching her jaw and grinding her teeth.

Entering the corporate world, the long hours at the computer and driving to see clients further stressed her jaw, and she also developed a pain 'like a knife wedged under the shoulder blade'. The only way to survive the day was to have a Voltaren injection. By her late twenties, Vanessa found herself exhausted, dreading facing each new day, and the fit, sporty enthusiastic girl she had been was a distant memory.

Her BSR journey was a process of first unlocking the tension stored throughout her back and neck, restoring efficient nerve supply, and only then could the body stress in her jaw be addressed. After the jaw tension was released it unlocked for the first time in eight years. The hip problem disappeared along with the shoulder-blade pain, as well as her lower-back ache. Vanessa had the sense of rediscovering her real self. This case shows that it is essential to deal with the body as a mechanical whole, as all structures are interconnected.

Note: If jaw stress keeps recurring after BSR, there may be an unbalanced bite involving the teeth, and a dentist should be consulted.

Loss of the sense of smell

For no apparent reason, a woman of fifty-seven suddenly lost her sense of smell. About a year later, while she had a cold with a congested nose and sinus headache, she had a BSR session. Body stress was released on the bones of the skull and face, and over her jaw. When she arrived home she blew her nose and 'two hard balls of mucus came out, one from each nostril'. She was immediately aware that her sense of smell was back.

Body stress in a tooth socket

There have been several cases of people with unrelenting pain in a tooth, who have asked if BSR could help in some way. Naturally they had been thoroughly examined by their dentists, and no problem could be detected on X-ray. A stress test was done by pressing lightly in specific directions on the face, over the tooth. The body's response indicated the line of tension, which was then released in the opposite direction. Because the pain subsided, one may conclude that the cause was pressure from tension in the ligaments which hold the tooth in the socket, possibly from hard or uneven biting.

Daily nosebleeds

An eighty-nine-year-old woman had been undergoing BSR for several months, when she told her practitioner that she would like to share a secret. Every day of her life, as far back as she could remember, she had woken with a nosebleed. She had accepted it as a normal part of life. But after her fourth session it abruptly stopped happening. She had waited until now to talk about it, to ensure that it was not just a temporary piece of magic.

Arms and hands

As the nerve supply to the arms and hands originates from the spinal nerves of the neck, it is essential that any body stress in the neck is released. In many instances, pain, stiffness and numbness in the arm or hand is due to compression in the neck and not to body stress in the arm itself.

The shoulder joint

The upper-arm bone fits into a shallow socket on the side of the shoulder blade. As this allows a wide range of motion, the shoulder joint is easily stressed. Reaching above the head, stretching the arm backwards, jarring effects in sports like tennis – these actions may strain the ligaments and muscles of the shoulder, and tension becomes locked into the joint.

The shoulder may be stiff and painful. If there is a build-up of inflammation the pain may be intense. In this case the release of the body stress would most likely have to be carried out several times over a period of time, to enable the joint to stabilise and healing to take place.

In a long-term case of body stress, the shoulder may become 'frozen', i.e. its mobility is severely restricted. In certain such cases, full movement of the joint is restored within hours of the stress being released. In others this occurs only after several sessions. For two years a forty-five-year-old housewife had not been able to raise her right arm or use it to carry anything. The shoulder had locked up immediately after lunging over to the back seat of the car to smack a disobedient child. Body stress was released in the shoulder joint, as well as in the spine. Immediately after her session, she went shopping, and while carrying the grocery bags out to the car she suddenly became aware that she was carrying them with her right arm. The shoulder ached over the next two BSR sessions, as full sensation returned, then eased completely.

The elbow, wrist and hand

These joints may be stressed by jarring the arm, as in a fall, by twisting movements, such as using a screwdriver or opening a tight jar, or by vigorous actions like scrubbing or sawing.

Tension may become locked into the elbow joint, between the small wrist bones, or between the hand bones. Carrying heavy shopping with

the handles looped around the fingers may induce body stress in the joints of the fingers or at the knuckles.

Pain or stiffness will be experienced, and possibly numbness or tingling. There may be weakness of the muscles when attempting to lift or grasp an object.

Hand restriction

A pianist was aware of a sense of restriction in the palm area of one hand. Body stress was located between the hand bones. A few days after the releases, he found that the reach of his hand had increased, enhancing his skill in playing the piano.

An old wrist injury

For six months Rita, a woman in her sixties, had been undergoing regular BSR, as her neck and shoulder area had been stiff and painful for nearly forty years. She traced her problems back to a fall from a horse when she was sixteen. The day came when she reported that her neck was fully moveable and pain-free, but she held up her left hand. 'My wrist is so painful I can hardly use it, though I haven't done anything to injure it.' She remembered that after the fall in her teens the wrist had been 'agony' for two weeks, then all the pain had cleared up. But it had been rigid ever since.

The BSR tests showed stress patterns across the joints of the wrist bones and the forearm. A week after the releases, Rita phoned to say, 'This is incredible – not only has all the pain gone, but my wrist is flexible again, for the first time since I was sixteen.'

It appears that, with the long-term body stress in the neck, the nerve supply to the wrist had been disrupted all that time. When the pressure in the neck was released, sensation was restored to the wrist, which had obviously also been stressed in the fall from the horse. When the local stress was released, the body was able, even after all that time, to restore normal function in the wrist. She was amazed to realise her body had 'buried' that stress for all those years, and she lost no time in fulfilling a lifelong ambition – she took up golf.

> ### Instead of cortisone
>
> Dave was an illustrator and musician, but a 'frozen' shoulder had put his life on hold. The shoulder was immobile, he could not hold a guitar, and his neck was painful. His GP recommended a cortisone injection, but Dave hoped to avoid this and chose to undergo BSR instead. After his first session, in which body stress was released in the neck and lower back, some movement was restored and he was able to do some drawing. By the third session he was feeling pain in the elbow and thumb, and tension was released in these structures. This shows that the nerves in the neck which supply the arm had been decompressed. After a total of seven sessions all Dave's pain had cleared up, 95 per cent of the shoulder movement was restored, and he was back to work and playing the guitar.

Legs and feet

As the nerve supply to the legs and feet originates from the spinal nerves of the lower back, it is vital that any body stress in this area of the spine is released.

The hip joint

The ball-shaped structure at the upper end of the thigh bone fits into a deep, secure socket in the pelvis. However, this joint may be stressed by movements such as mounting a bicycle or a horse, or in a fall, or from sitting cross-legged when unaccustomed to this position.

As tension becomes locked into the hip joint there may be restricted mobility, a sharp jabbing pain deep in the joint, or a milder ache when walking or dancing. People often describe it as feeling like the leg is falling off. The pain usually eases almost immediately after the release.

A 'shortened' hip tendon

At sixty-six, Greta had pain in her groin and hip joint which became so intense when lying down that she could no longer sleep at all. After X-rays of the hip she was told that 'a tendon had become too short' and an operation was advised, even though it was described as risky. The surgery was scheduled to be performed in eleven weeks' time.

The diagnosis did not seem logical to Greta, as she had been aware of the hip pain developing slowly, ever since a knee operation several years before. She decided to try BSR as she had the sense that the tendon was not shortened, but rather 'blocked' in some way.

She explained to the practitioner that she also had lower-back pain at times, as well as limited movement in her neck. Body stress was released in her spine and hip joint, and after two sessions the lower-back pain escalated. After the fourth session, although the hip and groin pain at night persisted, the groin ache eased off during the day. The sixth session resulted in the miracle of being able to sleep again.

As only slight hip pain remained Greta took the decision to cancel the surgery. She went off on a winter holiday, and even risked skiing, with no ill effects. As at times she felt some lower-back stiffness she continued having a BSR session once every three months.

The knee joint

This joint undergoes a great deal of daily strain, as not only does it bear the weight of the body, it is designed for the flexibility of a hinge joint. The cartilage pad in the knee and the ligaments supporting the joint may be stressed by twisting the knee, by jarring it in a fall, or in giving a hard kick.

Besides being painful, the knee joint may be weakened to the point of collapsing when pressure is exerted on the leg, as in going up or down stairs.

The ankle and foot

Body stress may become locked into the joints if a person jars or twists the ankle, as in stepping off a pavement incorrectly, or as the result of a kicking action. In addition to pain, there may be the sensation of the ankle giving way when the weight of the body is placed on that leg. The joints of the toes may also become stressed and this may in time contribute to the development of a bunion – a distortion in the area of the big toe.

An old ankle injury

A woman in her fifties fractured an ankle bone, and two years later it was still swollen and stiff, although there was no pain. In addition, she was experiencing lower-back pain and an ache in the back of her thigh. After body stress was released in the spine over several sessions, the back and leg pain withdrew. No stress was detectable in her ankle. A month later she returned and reported that her ankle had become painful. Stress was located and detected in the ankle and heel regions. By the following day the swelling, which had been present for two years, had subsided, and the foot was fully flexible and free of pain. It is significant that the tension stored in the ankle could be detected and dealt with only once efficient nerve supply to the area had been restored.

CHAPTER 10

The Body Stress Release consultation

Body Stress Release is carried out in a professional setting, in a private consulting room. The practitioner takes a case history, making notes on past accidents, fractures and operations, as well as establishing what the client is experiencing at present. Questions may be asked about exercise and sports, and posture relating to occupation. This information helps the practitioner gain a broad view of the client's life.

The practitioner gives a brief explanation of how BSR works, to dispel any misconceptions and show that the technique does not involve anything mysterious or mystical.

Most people choose to consult a BSR practitioner when seeking pain relief, especially for lower-back, leg, shoulder and neck pain and headaches. These complaints are noted, as they may provide insights as to where the tension may be stored in the body. However, the practitioner ensures that the client understands that BSR does not involve the diagnosis or treatment of any condition, thus it does not in any way replace medical care.

A BSR session varies in length, depending on what the assessment shows. It may take as little as ten minutes, or up to half an hour or longer. As BSR is a process, initially three appointments are made for a new client. Then, depending on the body's response to the releases, the client is advised regarding follow-up appointments.

The assessment

While fully clothed, the client lies face down on a padded table, or is lowered on a specially designed BSR couch – this is comfortable for people who, through injury or infirmity, have difficulty climbing onto a raised surface.

The practitioner activates the biofeedback mechanism of the body by moving the feet in a very specific way, 'like windscreen wipers', one client commented. This procedure is called 'the monitor'. The practitioner then does a series of body stress tests, pressing lightly on various points in specific directions.

If there is body stress present at a site, this very slightly irritates the nervous system, which reacts with a tiny withdrawal reflex. This response

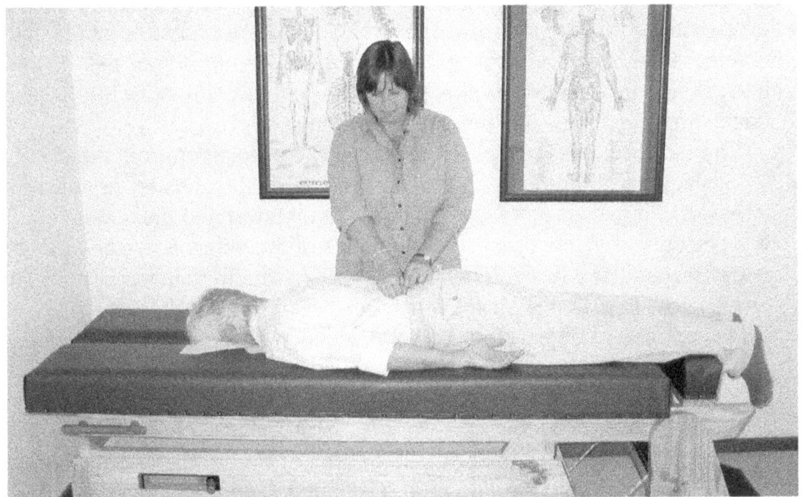

A Body Stress Release session, using the specially designed couch

lasts for several seconds, which allows the practitioner to carry out the 'monitor' manoeuvre, and observe a small, temporary shortening of one leg. If there is no stress at the site tested, then there will be no muscular response. The sensitivity of this process enables the practitioner to detect even minute sites of body stress.

The body's 'secret' information

It is the body's intelligence that indicates the precise location and direction of the lines of tension. It is not the practitioner making an educated guess, or an intellectual deduction, based on painful spots or tight muscles, as this may be misleading. By consulting the body's wisdom in this way, the practitioner receives information and guidance that may not be accessible in other ways.

To illustrate this: a woman of forty-two had experienced almost constant pain between her shoulder blades for several years. She had many different forms of treatment in that area, such as massage, spinal manipulation, hot and cold packs and anti-inflammatory cream applied to the muscles. Nothing brought relief. In the BSR assessment, her body's 'monitor' indicated that there was a small site of body stress between her shoulder blades, but a great deal of tension was stored in her lower back, even though she was not aware of any pain there. The intense compression of the nerves in the lumbar spine had caused the long muscles of the back to tighten, resulting in the ache in her upper back. After the lower-back stress was released, the shoulder-blade pain faded.

The testing process does not require any co-operation from the client, who simply lies there and relaxes. The BSR practitioner is trained intensively in this art of 'reading' the body's responses to the stress tests. It is so subtle that most clients are unaware of the irritation reaction of the body. Because of this some people may think it is a mysterious or magical procedure, whereas it is a simple neuromuscular reaction from the body – working on the same principle as the knee-jerk reflex test done by doctors.

The release

After locating the stress patterns in an area of the body, the practitioner carries out the releases. A firm prod or stimulus is applied, usually with the thumb, on the multiple spots involved, in the correct directions. This has

the effect of initiating an organised sequence of messages to the brain, alerting it to the stored tension. The brain can then send commands to the structures concerned to release it. Thus, although the practitioner's actions set the process in motion, the release is effected by the body's own wisdom. As the process is so precise, it does not require much force to provide the stimulus that will relay an awareness of the stressed area to the brain. So the pressure applied in the releases is quite light.

Clients often comment that it feels so gentle that they are amazed that it is such an effective technique. A large, tough Western Cape farmer was persuaded by his wife to have BSR as he had experienced quite severe lower-back pain for many years. After the session he told her that the process felt so gentle that he was convinced nothing had been done, and that he was the victim of a confidence trick. The next morning she could not suppress her amusement when he woke with such aching in his back that he felt he had been 'run over by a truck'. Nerve pathways that had been partially numbed for years came back into operation all at once. This dynamic response convinced him that something was happening, and he saw the process through until all the back pain had withdrawn.

The secret lies in the precision – the practitioner performs the releases on the exact sites and in the directions indicated by the body's responses. As the body is designed to be tension-free, it requires little force to return to normal – it will very easily use the energy provided to bring about the unlocking of stored stress. By contrast, it took a great deal of force to lock the stress in, from incorrect use or an accident. Obviously, if a person is experiencing intense pain, the releases on certain sites may feel sensitive or even painful.

In BSR we realise 'more is not better' – the application of a stimulus along a line of stress does not need to be forceful, but simply accurate. If too much force is applied to the body, it could aggravate a stressed area, causing muscles to tighten further in a defensive, armouring reaction.

The immediate effects

Often the client is aware of instant relaxation of tight muscles, improved mobility and reduced pain. The practitioner may observe flattening of ridges of muscles in the back or neck, and increased flexibility in the ankles. It often happens that people step onto the couch with the back in a painful spasm, and after the releases they step off with the spine completely straight again.

Safety

A wonderful security is built into the BSR procedure. As the force applied is light enough never to override the body's natural protective resistance, if an inaccurate stimulus was applied, the body would simply reject it. No harm would be done – it would merely be ineffective.

The explanation

After the releases, the practitioner explains the relevance of the sites of body stress to the client, using charts to link cause and effect, e.g. a person with numb hands can see on a nerve chart the connections from the painful lower neck to the hands. A comment frequently made by clients is, 'This is so logical – why has no one explained this to me before?' They often express relief that their 'mysterious' problem may have a straightforward explanation.

At each session, the practitioner updates the client on the changes that are occurring. In BSR we believe it is important for clients to understand what is being done – after all, it is their body. In addition, when people understand a situation, they are more motivated to follow advice and take responsibility for their well-being.

In severe, long-term cases, being kept informed about the meaning of what they are experiencing keeps the clients from despairing. When they finally reach the hoped-for destination of their journey back to health, they express their gratitude at having been talked through the process.

The sceptic who did not give up

Jonathan described his many years of back pain as excruciating. He was forty-nine, a builder, and had sustained several spinal fractures in landmine traumas – in the neck, mid back and lower back. His left knee locked up in a bent position when he walked, and his right leg alternated between numbness and burning. He also had shoulder-joint pain. Over many BSR sessions during the next seven months the sensations in the different areas varied; just as certain ones improved, others became much worse. He had grave doubts as to whether the releases were doing him any good, and he would have given up if the practitioner had not explained what was happening.

When the pain was finally receding, Jonathan made the mistake of lifting a large pot with his back twisted. For a while he experienced agony, but several sessions later he turned the corner. Two years after he began, he reached the point of only a little back pain, and more general flexibility and mobility. He joked with his practitioner that no matter what he was feeling, she told him it was 'wonderful'. If there was more pain, she reassured him that communication was being restored. When there was no pain, she told him healing was taking place. He reached the point where he could laugh at whatever he was experiencing, and see how it was another step in the journey.

Advice to the client

Depending on the findings, the practitioner may give the client some guidance on how to maximise the benefit of the BSR sessions, and avoid the recurrence of body stress. This may involve advice on correct sitting, bending, etc., and modifying an exercise programme. In a severe case, the client may be advised to stop vigorous exercise or sport for a time, to allow the body to adapt and heal.

A man in his thirties assured his BSR practitioner that he had given up his toe-touching exercises, in order to allow his lower back to settle down. About six sessions later, there was no decrease in his lower-back pain and he stopped coming for releases.

> BSR is not opposed to exercise, only to actions that go against the body's design …

Months later he reappeared. He said he had consulted a specialist as his feet had started to go numb, and he was told his back may require surgery. He then confessed that he had lied about his exercise programme – he had not stopped his toe-touching exercises. After three sessions, full feeling had returned to his feet and his back was pain-free.

BSR is not opposed to exercise, only to actions that go against the body's design and cause unnecessary stress. The client may be shown specific exercises for toning the lower back and abdominal muscles, and some self-help procedures for the neck.

CHAPTER 11

After the releases

As pressure is released from nerves, there may be immediate relief from pain, relaxing of tight muscles, even straightening of distorted posture. Usually this is the case if the body stress has occurred recently – the process of restoring normal tone is very rapid, and the life energy flow is quickly re-established.

If the body stress has been present for a long time, it will be necessary for a number of stress releases to be carried out over a period of time. This allows the layers of tightened muscles to relax progressively back to their normal tone. This process of unlocking the deeply stored tension could be compared to peeling away the layers of an onion.

Increased function, energy and well-being

With reduced nerve compression, there is improved communication, which results in improved function of organs. Clients often report that certain conditions that they had not mentioned have cleared up, such as constipation, bladder problems, indigestion, etc. Usually the physical changes are accompanied by an emotional upliftment.

As the muscles lock up in layers, like a protective corset, the body's energy is diverted into holding the muscles in this defensive mode, resulting in constant tiredness. As the body stress is released, the muscles resume their normal supportive role and more energy is available for living.

Getting in tune with life

André is a violin maker and musician, and at fifty-eight he displayed many traits of an intensely creative personality. As tautly strung as his instruments, he was vital and alert, but also jittery and hypersensitive. His BSR practitioner described his attitude to life as constant 'fight or flight', and his neck and shoulders were rock hard. Two years before he had had a total breakdown, physically and emotionally. After the release sessions, he was shaky and exhausted and had a headache. But one change encouraged him to keep on – his arm felt freer, and he could play the cello again. After the third time, André had a new awareness of his body – his walking was more flowing, his neck and shoulders felt more relaxed as he worked on crafting violins, and he was sleeping well. Two visits later he had a panic attack, followed by the realisation that his periods of depression were shorter and his thinking less rigid. This led to a whole new perception of his life. His fears about making a living dissolved, and he no longer felt he had to put on a false show of confidence. He was able to 'let life happen' without struggling feverishly. As the compression came out of his body, the emotional pressure let go of his mind as well.

From negative to positive

At sixty-five, Norman was irritable, sceptical, and generally negative about life. Not surprising, as he had to contend with intense lower-back pain, was forced to use a walking stick, and felt worn out. He was reluctant to try BSR, as he believed nothing could undo the ravages of age, but his daughter eventually convinced him to see a practitioner.

Over the first three sessions, the pain withdrew in stages and Norman gave up his walking stick. He was greatly cheered by the realisation that, by using his back correctly, he could prevent the lower-back problem from recurring.

He eagerly followed all the advice he was given, and went shopping to find a lounge suite that would honour his spine's biomechanical design. He also resolved to cut down on the commitments in his life and start enjoying himself. He was able to return to his favourite activity, cycling. Norman described his transformation by saying he felt he was coming back to the core of being who he was.

A BSR practitioner has collected some memorable quotations from her clients:

- A forty-year-old businessman asked: 'Do you sell bumper stickers … "Old man getting younger"?'
- Another businessman of thirty-eight: 'I couldn't get here quick enough; I feel as if I am going to be recharged, like a plug in a socket.'
- A housewife of thirty-nine: 'The whole family benefits from my having BSR. I am in a much better mood and can cope far more efficiently. In fact, my husband insists that I come to you.'
- Another housewife of thirty-four: 'Life is more colourful.'
- A fifteen-year-old girl: 'I feel so good I feel like I am gliding.'
- A computer programmer of thirty-six: 'I no longer feel trapped in my body.'
- Another programmer of thirty-seven: 'I no longer respond to stress from a high or low perspective, I merely glide through it.'
- A thirty-year-old businesswoman: 'I am really worried. I am just not worrying about anything any more.'
- A staff member of a health centre: 'People look miserable in the waiting room; after coming out of the BSR practice room they are all smiley – what happens in there?'

The process of healing

It could be said that healing is usually a process, not an event.

Why does pain come and go?

When pressure is released from nerve pathways, there may be an increase in pain for a while as sensation is restored to partially numbed nerves.

As the healing progresses, the irritation to the nerve drops below its firing point, and there is the wonderful sense of pain receding. However, while the process is ongoing, it is quite easy to irritate the nerve back up to firing point, for example sitting incorrectly or for too long may cause pressure in the lower back, and it starts to ache again. If one avoids the stressful action, it allows the nerve irritability to once again drop below threshold level.

This is why it is essential to allow the body time to complete its healing, before challenging it with stressful activities. Runners are sometimes advised to do brisk walking and then alternate walking with short runs, before going back into running races.

A keen golfer with intense lower-back pain hobbled into the BSR practice. The next day he woke up pain-free, and was so excited that he ignored the advice to rest until the next session. Instead he pursued his passion and went to the golf course. As he hit his first ball, his twisted lower back went into spasm and his legs gave in. His golfing partners carried him off the course. At his next BSR session he agreed to allow his body time for the miracle of self-healing to take place, and to improve his muscle tone before going full tilt back into golf.

Increased sensation or sensitivity

As the energy flow is restored, some people may initially experience sensations of tingling or warmth. In certain cases there may be increased pain for a short time, as feeling is restored to numbed nerves. This is a healing pain.

Imagine jamming your finger in a car door – you may feel no pain until the door is opened. Pressure comes off the finger and sensation floods into the numbed area. Feeling and communication are restored, and healing can begin.

A woman of fifty-two had a long history of lower-back and neck pain. She had been diagnosed with osteoarthritis in both areas of the spine, and had undergone surgery to a lumbar disc. When she came for BSR she had spasms of pain in her shoulders, aching in one arm, and frequent pain in one hip and knee. Her posture was stooped and she looked exhausted. The practitioner found body stress not only in the spine, but in the shoulders and knees, and over her chest, face and skull. Over the first two sessions the pain escalated in her arms and legs and over her coccyx, and the tops of her feet felt bruised. However, she understood that healing is a process and was determined to see it through. By the third session her posture had improved and her face was glowing. Over two further sessions the pains returned, but at a lesser intensity, and then withdrew.

Temporary stiffness

It sometimes occurs that after the releases a person may feel an area stiffen up for a few days. The body's wisdom is directing the surface muscles to tighten, in order to restrict mobility. In this way there is minimal irritation to the underlying tissues during their healing process.

Tiredness

After a BSR session, some people may experience a sense of tiredness. This means the body is going rapidly into the self-healing process, and as energy is diverted into managing this situation, the person may feel a strong need for sleep. Of course it would be most beneficial to co-operate with the body, and to rest or sleep so that it can get on with its work.

Ongoing upgrading

The effect of BSR is to improve the communication between the brain and the cells of the body, thereby assisting the body to restore normal function. Over the years we have observed how this is an ongoing process.

In Ewald's case, after several years of having regular releases, he noticed many signs that his body was upgrading itself, besides the relief from pain and stiffness. One day he realised that besides being able to curl under, his toes could spread apart, something he had never been able

to do. Then he started becoming aware of feeling in his kneecaps – they had been numb his whole life.

Recently he complained that his shoes had become too small and were pinching his feet. He realised that he now had full sensation restored to his feet. All his life he had worn very tight shoes which helped him to be more aware of his feet, so that he could walk feeling his feet touching the ground, without looking down. He had to invest in a new wardrobe of shoes in a larger size.

Another change that occurred was that the frequent itch he had had between his shoulder blades was gone.

The removal of 'armour'

Clients often comment that BSR has freed them from a sense of rigidity or general body stiffness. A dancer felt as though she had removed armour-plating from her chest. She felt straighter and lighter, and more open to other people. For a time she had a sense of being vulnerable, as her 'armouring' had provided an emotional defence against the world.

Reversing and uncovering the past

Another remarkable effect of releasing body stress is seen in certain cases. After several sessions a client may say, 'I now feel a pain in my back identical to what I felt after I fell off a horse when I was seventeen', or, 'My ankle has started to ache – I injured it twenty years ago.' As these areas are 'rewired' or reconnected at a deep level to the brain, it seems to awaken the brain's awareness of them, and the body can finally heal the 'buried' injury.

As healing progresses, it is as though the body rejuvenates – joints regain mobility that had been lost in a past accident. The body is able to take action to deal with old injuries which had not been fully healed, which it had been holding 'in storage'.

The resurfacing of Ewald's original injury

Ewald underwent a very dramatic experience of a deep injury from the distant past being 'brought to the surface' for healing. About a year after his lower-back problem had cleared up, we were on holiday,

playing a very amateur game of tennis. After hitting the ball, he suddenly felt a wrenching pain tear through his chest and he staggered and bent over double. He felt like all the air had been forced out of his lungs. In that moment he had a flashback of his father carrying the five-year-old Ewald, straight after the fall from the tree – his chest muscles were in spasm and he could scarcely breathe.

He had to spend the next few days lying face down on a bed, with his chest draped over a pile of pillows. I released stress over the thoracic spine several times each day. Then he was able to lie flat, but it took a week before all the chest pain withdrew.

He was amazed to find that, after this episode, his breathing felt easier than he had ever experienced. It was as though a constricting band had been removed from around his ribs, and he realised he had always accepted his rather shallow breathing as normal.

An old fracture

Andrea, aged thirty, had been diagnosed with a spondylolisthesis in her lower back. This is a forward shift of a vertebra due to a defect of the joints that bind it to the adjacent vertebrae. Besides lower-back pain, she had sciatica in the left leg, her knees ached and moved with a grinding sensation, and her right shoulder was sore. She had a history of injuries, having been a ballet dancer for twenty-one years, and she had fallen down stairs onto her coccyx and fractured her right collarbone a few years ago.

The BSR practitioner was startled to see Andrea's posture when she arrived for her second session – her back was bent to one side, and her shoulder girdle was pulled into a spasm to the right. Andrea was not concerned – she said her spine had gone into the identical con-figuration at the time of the collarbone break, and she had the sense that her body was in the process of accessing and healing the residue of this trauma. Two sessions later, her posture was straight again, all the pain had faded to tenderness, and her whole body felt lighter.

Emotional release

As human beings we are made up of three aspects – body, mind and emotions. These are, of course, interconnected and interdependent. When we have a physical experience, it also affects us mentally and emotionally; something that has a mental or emotional impact will also reverberate into the body. The emotion becomes locked into the physical structure, constricting the life energy flow. The physical stress then perpetuates or reinforces the emotional reaction that introduced the stress into the body. By releasing the body stress the individual is enabled to experience facing life without emotional armouring, and will be more relaxed and less defensive in responding to life.

Scientists did an intriguing experiment with spiders. After feeding them with blood from depressed people, the webs they spun were irregular and fragmented. This implies that the people's body chemistry had been altered by their psychological state. It is also known that depression lowers the immune system – there is a decrease in the number of disease-fighting white blood cells.

Because of the interconnection of the body, mind and emotions, when body stress is present, not only are there physical effects, but one's mental and emotional well-being are also undermined.

After the physical tension is released, some people become aware of greater mental clarity. Others feel an emotional lightness, or a surge of enthusiasm for life, as energy levels rise.

A burden lifted

Belinda, a student of twenty-two, decided to try BSR to ease her shoulder tension and mild lower-back ache. She had no idea the physical releases would result in a psychological transformation. As body stress in her diaphragm was released, she felt a surge of emotion in her solar plexus, and she could not hold back a flood of tears. At the end of the session she had the sense that a great burden had been lifted. Months later, this lightness continued. When thinking about what happened, her logical mind told her the weight she had been carrying

around dated back to her parents' divorce twelve years before. As a defensive mechanism, she had tightened her shoulders and diaphragm, and when these muscles released their tension, the suppressed sorrow spontaneously let go at the same time.

Stored shock

Sometimes a person may undergo a spontaneous surfacing of stored shock during the BSR session. In this case, as the physical tension releases, there is an emotional letting go. The person may become very cold and shiver and tears may flow as there is a reconnecting with some traumatic experience from the past.

A memory may suddenly arise – an accident, a loss, a fright – it may even be something totally forgotten. In these rare cases, the practitioner covers the client with a blanket, reassuring him or her that they are in a safe place, and it is good to let the emotions out.

Clients who have had this experience have spoken of an enormous weight being removed, or of the release of a long-buried hurt or fear that was limiting their life. The practitioner may suggest to some clients that they see a professional counsellor, if they feel the need for guidance in talking over and working through the emotional trauma.

A businesswoman in her forties came for BSR hoping for relief from back and neck pain. After several sites of body stress had been released she was overcome with emotion. She was amazed to find herself feeling all the shock and sorrow she had gone through at age twelve, when her father had died. At her second session she said she felt transformed – the emotions she had been suppressing all those years had surfaced and been released.

Dizziness

Occasionally a client may feel slight dizziness on standing upright at the end of the BSR session. The sensation disappears after sitting for a minute or two. This light-headedness is due to the releases having restored communication between the brain and proprioceptors – these are specialised sensory nerve endings which provide spatial information about where the body is in space, and which are vital for balance. As the

flood of extra information reaches the brain, it needs a few minutes to compute it.

Unexpected emotions

When a long-term health problem is cleared very suddenly, a person may react with unexpected emotions.

A man of thirty-four arrived for his second appointment looking confused and angry. 'This doesn't make any sense. My neck has been stiff and painful for years. How can it get fixed in just one session?' He rotated his head from side to side. 'It's completely free again. How could it be put right so easily?'

After several BSR sessions a woman in her fifties was free of pain, mobility had returned to her spine, and she no longer needed to wear a steel-lined corset. Along with her amazed relief at being set free from this cage, she expressed a sense of bitterness. 'For thirty years I've had to wear that corset – I was told that my lower back would collapse without it. If only I had been able to do this back then, my whole life would have been different.'

Another woman in her fifties felt sorrow and loss when her lower-back pain had been resolved. 'I always wanted another baby, but I was told that it would be disastrous to get pregnant with my back problem. I feel cheated – I know now I could have had that third child.'

Body awareness

Tension may have been stored in the body for a long period. With the release of body stress, for the first time a person may have full awareness of his or her physical being. Ewald tells clients that they are having their first 'in body' experience. They become more able to recognise what their body is communicating regarding its needs – posture, rest, exercise, diet, etc.

After several BSR sessions, a man in his forties discovered he had lost his desire for red meat. He remarked wistfully that his favourite treat had been steak and chops, cooked on the barbecue, but acknowledged that he now had no choice but to follow the wisdom of his body.

CHAPTER 12

Who needs Body Stress Release, and when?

No one can deny that being alive in a physical body is a stressful experience. Some stresses are avoidable, some manageable, and some are beyond our control.

As everyone will at some time be subjected to stress overload, Body Stress Release is of benefit to everyone. Because of its gentle approach, it is suitable for all ages, from newborn babies to the aged, and for people in all states of health.

After surgery

Undergoing surgery is a stressful experience: chemically, from the anaesthesia and medication; emotionally; and mechanically, as a result of being lifted and turned, and lying for long periods.

The BSR practitioner obviously does not work over the area that has been operated on, but tests for stored tension at adjacent and related sites.

In some cases the procedure has to be adapted to suit the client's condition. A woman who underwent a hysterectomy woke up from the operation with severe neck pain and headache. As she could not lie on her abdomen, her upper-back and neck tension were released while she was sitting up in her hospital bed.

An elderly man experienced upper- and lower-back pain after a major chest operation. He stood with his arms braced against a wall while the releases were carried out.

> Because of its gentle approach, it is suitable for all ages … and people in all states of health.

Spinal surgery

If back pain is not relieved after disc surgery, a person usually believes the surgery was a failure, and no improvement can be expected – a case of learn to live with the pain and limitations. However, the surgery may have achieved its objective: the removal of the disc bulge has taken pressure off the spinal nerves. So why is there still pain? This is because the injury which caused the prolapsed disc also resulted in tension locking into the entire lower back, therefore it is very likely that there is body stress, causing nerve irritation, above or below, or even over the sites of the surgery.

Alec, a technician aged forty-eight, is the essence of an action man, whose passions are sailing, diving and skydiving. His adventurous lifestyle took its toll on his spine, and he had to undergo three laminectomies – disc surgery in the lower back. However, the pain in his lower back remained intense, and he had a numb foot. The only way he could cope with his active life was to take six to ten painkillers a day.

He came to BSR with a specific goal – to go on a three-day sailing trip without having to take any painkilling or anti-inflammatory medication. With his history, he accepted that it would most likely be a long process to unlock all the stored compression in his back. He had

a BSR session at two-weekly intervals, over eleven months. Gradually, the rigid muscles of his whole spine relaxed, nerve pressure diminished, and he reduced the medication. The back muscles became balanced and his flexibility returned. Finally Alec's patience and determination paid off and he achieved his objective – he led his four-man crew on the planned voyage without medication.

In another case of surgery, a seventy-five-year-old woman had two laminectomies in her lumbar spine. With a distorted posture, she had to use a walking stick and took eight to ten painkillers each day at two- to four-hourly intervals in order to cope with the back pain. After ten BSR sessions the pressure in the spine had withdrawn to the point that she could dispense with the walking stick, and reduce the pain medication to only two or three per day. Her practitioner says she literally started skipping in for her session.

After an accident

Any trauma, whether caused by a car accident, a fall, or some other violent event, is likely to result in body stress. If it is not released, as time passes the layers of muscles in the back and neck will become increasingly tense, in order to minimise mobility and avoid further tissue damage. It makes sense to have the locked-in tension dealt with as soon as possible.

A thirty-six-year-old woman describes her experience of a major car accident: 'On the freeway my car was hit by a drunken driver who had lost control of his vehicle. He collided with the driver's door and front wing of my car, causing it to roll onto its roof. Luckily it landed in a gully full of bushes which acted as a cushion and probably saved my life. I was suspended upside down by my seat-belt, but managed to free myself and crawl out of the car. Besides feeling frozen with shock I had immense pain in my hip and could hardly put any weight on that leg.

Two-and-a half-hours later I was taken to a BSR practitioner. I felt extremely dizzy while being lowered on the couch. The pain on my right side was quite intense, and my back and neck were worked on very gently but thoroughly. My ankles were very stiff to begin with, then gradually I felt them become looser. I dreaded waking up the next day, but after very little sleep I found I could walk fairly well and only experienced pain and discomfort when sitting down or getting in and out of a car. After my second appointment three days later I was amazed at the speed of my recovery. It just proves that by getting attended to as quickly as possible you speed up the healing process, by not allowing the trauma to be locked in.'

After a stroke

In BSR there have been a number of cases of individuals who had undergone a stroke and had persisting effects, such as paralysis of the muscles of the face or limbs. In these cases body stress was released along the spine. In many cases there was marked increase of mobility of the limbs and improvement of speech. This indicates that there was some restoration of communication in nerve pathways to and from the brain.

Wheelchair-bound people

- *Paraplegics*, who are paralysed from the waist down, subject their arms, shoulders and neck muscles to strain as they propel their wheelchair and lift themselves onto beds and into cars. They often feel pain in these areas, sometimes with headaches. Regular BSR can help prevent the stress from accumulating, and assist in maintaining muscle strength.
- *Quadriplegics*: when a person is paralysed from the neck down, is it possible that releasing tension stored in the spine could provide some benefit? Some BSR cases suggest that, even though the spinal cord has been damaged, certain nerve pathways are still capable of transmitting impulses if pressure on the cord or spinal nerves is reduced.

As a result of a car accident in which his spinal cord was crushed, a young man was paralysed from the lower neck downwards. He had lost all use of his arms and legs, and was held braced into the wheelchair. His neck muscles were so weak that his head was tilted down onto his chest.

After several sessions of BSR in which body stress was released in his neck, the muscles had strengthened and he held his head upright. This fact alone greatly improved the quality of his life, as he was able to look at people while talking to them. He also acquired some movement in one shoulder.

A woman who fractured her neck had no feeling from the neck down. Her body was in a twisted posture in her wheelchair, and she had such intense, constant head pain that her doctors were considering attaching a morphine pump to her body. Desperation led her to BSR, and over seven months many changes took place.

The permanent migraine lifted and she now experiences only the occasional 'ordinary' headache. Her posture has straightened. Some feeling has returned to one leg, and tingling is felt in the other. The legs used to be cold to the touch, and now are warm, as is her whole body, so blood circulation has improved. She is now aware of the practitioner working on her back. Most dramatic of all, movement has returned to her arms, and she can fully extend one arm above her head.

Babies and children

See Chapter 13.

Pregnancy and after

Towards the end of their pregnancy, clients often comment, 'This is the only place I can be comfortable lying on my stomach.' With pregnant women, cushions are placed above and below the bulge, and this support takes the pressure off the abdomen.

As pregnancy advances, there is increasing tension in the lower back, which is usually also referred upwards to the shoulder-blade area or the

neck. Besides relieving these aches and pains, BSR plays an important role in helping the body prepare itself for the birth. By minimising the compression in the lumbar spine, there is improved communication in the whole pelvic region.

Many women experience difficult births while they have back problems. After undergoing BSR care during the subsequent pregnancy, they have found the birth process much easier.

The mother of two children tells her story:

'In 1990 after the birth of my eldest son I experienced severe lower-back pain. It was triggered by the very difficult birth, but in retrospect I realise it was the result of a long-term untreated problem. I remembered spending many days in the past in bed with incapacitating pain, and being treated with painkillers and anti-inflammatories.

My gynaecologist recommended that I try Body Stress Release but I opted for a more conventional type of physical treatment. Six months later I was coping, using painkillers, but still had a burning back. I was given various 'back-strengthening' exercises. I learned to live with backache, believing it was unavoidable, as my mother has a chronic back problem and I was led to believe my condition was inherited.

Then in 1995 I fell pregnant with my second son and soon started experiencing severe backache again. My gynaecologist again recommended BSR, and I decided to try it. I experienced immediate relief. After my son was born I had two sessions of BSR and I was fine after that.'

Postnatal-diarrhoea: After the birth of her third child, a very large baby, a woman in her thirties started having diarrhoea, day and night. The problem disrupted her whole life, making it difficult to go anywhere. Medical tests were done on all the organs of the digestive system, but no cause could be pinpointed. After body stress was released in the lower back, the night diarrhoea stopped. Over several months, with regular BSR, the daytime problem gradually receded.

Sportspeople

Not only can BSR assist the body in its recovery from and prevention of injury, freedom from stored tension allows increased energy and flexibility, enhancing performance potential.

Golfers have experienced improved co-ordination, and surfers have commented on their balance being upgraded. A cricketer who had given up bowling because of restriction in his shoulder regained his skill after his neck stress was released.

In their enthusiasm for their sport, and driven by a competitive spirit, players may ignore tight muscles and stiff, aching joints, and determine to 'work through the pain'. However, that old saying, 'no pain, no gain', has long been discredited. Sportspeople should listen to the wisdom of the body, which is telling them to take a break and to have the stored tension dealt with. Surface muscles tighten over a site of compression, to restrict movement and 'splint' the area so that healing can occur. To override this and continue with the sport or exercise is to risk injury.

A fitness enthusiast feels stiffness, usually in her lower back. 'I need to loosen up,' she thinks, and goes to the gym for a vigorous workout. This may include exercises that potentially could stress the spine, such as full sit-ups, twists and full forward bending. After the exercise session her back feels more mobile, and she assumes she is now 'fixed'.

In fact, the stressful exercises may cause the deepest, short back muscles to lock up in a protective state, which allows the longer, superficial muscles to relax. So the person will feel more mobile for a while. However, the deep compression will be taking its toll, disturbing the nerve supply to the limbs and internal organs. The back may feel 'looser', but other problems will start arising. The hamstring muscles at the back of the thighs may tighten, or the knees may become unstable. Perhaps some digestive upset may occur.

There may be an abrupt end to the false sense of security that the back is fine. A small movement, such as a simple stretch to reach for something, or twisting to turn while sitting, causes a sudden lower-back spasm. The slightly stressful movement is the 'straw that breaks the camel's back' – it overrides the holding capacity of those locked-up deep muscles, and the longer, more superficial muscles are forced to tighten to limit mobility and prevent damage.

Running

A thirty-six-year-old man had a passion for running, and was hampered by tight hamstrings. He explained that he had to do repeated toe-touching every morning to try to stretch his 'short' hamstrings. He found it hard to believe when we explained that this repeated exercise was stressing his lower back, and thereby causing irritation to the nerves from the lumbar spine which supply the hamstrings, keeping them constantly tense. Eventually he was persuaded to give up the toe-touching, to allow his lower-back stress to be released, and normal communication restored to his leg muscles. He was amazed to find his hamstrings were no longer 'short'.

Cycling

A thirty-four-year-old cycling enthusiast explained that he had undergone years of both emotional and physical stress. After a particularly arduous cycling race he had shoulder and leg pain, and felt that his cycling was causing his back problem. A fellow cyclist told him about BSR. The practitioner detected body stress in his lower back, neck, shoulder and chest. After two sessions the only pain remaining was tension in his ribs. After the importance of posture was explained to him he adjusted his bicycle seat to allow his lower back to maintain its natural curve, and changed the handlebars to a position that lessened the contraction of his chest muscles. He said he could now ride for longer and faster without any discomfort. He was so grateful to the man who had referred him to BSR that he sent him an expensive new saddle for his racing cycle.

A vital fact for sports people: *You cannot tone or build strength into tense muscles.* So in order to maximise fitness, it makes sense first to have stored tension released and communication restored.

> You cannot tone or build strength into tense muscles.

BSR has helped athletes to enhance their fitness. Every year before competitions like cycle races and marathons, clients have BSR in order to boost their performance. A couple in their sixties, who had run the Comrades Marathon for years, always came for their 'tune up' before the big day.

The elderly

Older people often blame pain and malfunction on ageing, and 'learn to live with' their problems. When they talk about being too old to expect any improvement, we point out to them that (unless they have a skin condition) there are no unhealed sores on their skin. Just as the healing process continues on the surface, it remains active throughout the body. As BSR is gentle and precise, it is safely applied to aged, frail people.

A weak bladder

A man in his sixties had accepted that his boating days were over. He had stopped going fishing with a group of friends due to his embarrassing problem of needing to urinate frequently – he could not last even an hour on the boat. After several months of regular BSR for long-term lower-back pain, he discovered that the pressure and irritation in his bladder were gone. 'I thought I just had a weak bladder because of my age,' he said. He was delighted to be able to rejoin the fishing expeditions. It is significant that the nerve supply to the bladder originates from the lower spine.

Osteoarthritis

A woman in her seventies arrived at our practice with a very positive attitude. 'My X-rays show I'm riddled with arthritis,' she said. 'The doctors

say nothing can be done – but I know you're going to heal me.' I made sure she understood that any healing that may take place would be thanks to her body's powers. She readily accepted this, adding, 'The X-rays are just a picture – they're not me.' While I appreciated her optimism, I struggled to hide my doubt as her situation looked hopeless. The report stated that she had advanced osteoarthritis – degeneration of the vertebrae with many osteophytes, bony outgrowths, especially in the neck region. She had been in constant, increasing pain for years.

After two sessions her neck was more mobile and she was free of pain. 'I knew it would work,' she declared cheerfully. What an enormous lesson for me – never to make assumptions and never to start out with a negative attitude. We have seen many similar cases in which osteophytes appear to be encroaching on the spinal nerves where they exit between the vertebrae. The fact that the pain withdraws after the releases shows that in these cases the bony growths are not exerting pressure on the nerves. The pain is caused by the compression effect of the tension stored in the neck or back structures.

Leg pain

Even at ninety-six the body remembers how to heal. When Anita reached that age, she had such intense pain in her right leg (she had undergone a hip-joint replacement operation to that leg twenty years before) that she was crying as she was lowered onto the BSR couch. Her GP had given her painkillers and reminded her that she was an old lady, and aches and pains were to be expected. The releases in her lower back were carried out very gently, and she felt an immediate lightening of the pain. By her third and final session, she was pain-free and told the practitioner that he had performed a miracle. When he assured her that the healing was coming from within her own body, she looked at him with some puzzlement. According to her daughter, a regular client, the pain has not recurred.

Too painful to walk

A woman of eighty-three was brought to a BSR practice lying down in the back of a car. In the past she had fractured her lower back in a fall, and it had fused naturally. At times she had been bedridden for weeks. Now she could not walk because of the extreme pain down both legs into her heels, and numbness in her feet. Immediately after the first session she felt so much relief that she insisted her friend drive her straight to the shopping centre. There she grabbed a trolley, hung onto it, and shopped for two hours. Over the next few BSR sessions the pain level rose and fell, and finally reduced to the point that she could do her housework again.

Ninety years young

Jakob appeared decades younger than his eighty-nine years. Tall and upright, he enjoyed cycling and long daily walks. But the years seemed to catch up with him overnight when he had a hard fall off his bicycle. He looked bent and shrunken, and intense leg pain put an end to his walking. He told his family it felt like the end of his life had arrived. When his knee started aching, his GP told him his knees were 'worn out'. But to the doctor's surprise the knee looked fine on X-ray. However, a specialist saw something amiss in Jakob's lower back, but said that nothing could be done because of his advanced age.

Four months later Jakob found his way to BSR, and after one pain-free day, the pain started coming and going. The practitioner advised him not to sit in his favourite armchair, the kind that keeps the legs raised. In his zeal to do everything possible to help his back, Jakob gave the chair away. Nine months later he was back to walking for up to an hour, and once again he had the posture of a young man. At a general check-up the specialists marvelled at his good health. Now ninety, he is still driving a car, planning holiday trips and enjoying life.

Certain occupations

There are occupations that involve a great deal of mechanical stress. Besides those that are obviously physically demanding, such as manual labour, certain pursuits place specific stress on the body.

Musicians

In the days of the Cape Town Symphony Orchestra we often saw musicians at our practice.

The violinists experienced neck and shoulder pain, particularly if a piece involved a great deal of 'scrubbing' as they called it.

A clarinet player arrived for an emergency appointment. His elbow had 'seized up' and he had a solo performance that evening. Fortunately after the releases the nerve irritation subsided in time for him to play.

We met several visiting conductors who were experiencing lower-back pain and spasm after their long overseas flights. They gave us tickets for the performances, and we were gratified to see that after BSR they were able to wield their baton with dramatic verve.

Hairdressers

Hairdressers are subjected daily to all three categories of stress. Mechanically, they undergo strain standing for hours. Holding up and manipulating the hairdryer and brush could stress their upper back, shoulder, elbow and wrist joints. Their environment is filled with chemicals which affect some people adversely. On top of this, they have the emotional demands of dealing with some clients' unrealistic expectations, as well as serving as an informal counsellor to those who confide in them.

Dentists

Dentists spend their days sitting at a twisted angle, neck rotated, and arms held up tensely, as they work on their patients. They often suffer from lower-back, shoulder-blade and neck pain, as well as headaches. It must also be extremely stressful to appear calm while constantly dealing with nervous people who are anticipating that you are going to hurt them.

Computer work

Working at a computer all day may be draining. A woman in her fifties, a bookkeeper, felt constantly tired. Her hands ached at the end of the working day, she was sleeping badly and grinding her teeth. In addition she had sciatic pain in one leg, an aching neck and jaw, and frequent indigestion and constipation. Over three sessions her complaints diminished then withdrew. On her fourth appointment she said that her haemorrhoids had also cleared up and she was sleeping well. She is now more aware of her body and maintaining correct posture while working.

'Hopeless' cases

BSR practitioners often hear the comment from a new client, 'You're my last resort – I've tried everything.' In a sense this puts pressure on the practitioner, but at the same time it means that any slight improvement in a 'hopeless' client will uplift the quality of his or her life to some degree. We do not give people false hope, but we always remind them that, when communication within the body is restored, its inbuilt ability to heal itself is activated. Even in those cases which do not seem to respond to BSR there is the possibility that, with stored tension being released, there will be some upgrading of general function.

An executive of forty-eight was one of these 'last chance' cases. X-rays of his lower back showed marked degeneration, with narrowed disc spaces, and bony spurs on the vertebrae. As the pain in his hip and leg was unbearable, he was forced to take painkillers every day. In his BSR session he could not lie down at first, so the initial releases were done standing. Once he was lowered on the couch, the pain caused him to be drenched in sweat, and he could barely stand up again. The pain intensified over the next two days, and then started to come and go. After four more sessions, only the ankle remained sensitive. In time this sensation faded.

Animals

The focus of BSR is on improving the health of humans, but some practitioners do at times assist their clients by attending to their pets. Animals are also vulnerable to body stress from accidents and falls. It may be obvious that they are feeling pain, have limited mobility, or are suffering

from some malfunction, even though there is no medical cause discernible. Many cats, dogs and horses have been helped by having stored tension released.

The cat who was starving

Tammy, a luxurious white Persian, could not eat. She was obviously hungry and would go to her bowl, but she could only lick at the food. The cat was thoroughly examined by the vet, who thought something may be stuck in the throat, but nothing could be found. Tammy's owner tried to hand-feed her with soft food, but she could take in very little. Every day she grew thinner, and her owner felt helpless to stop her from starving to death.

A BSR practitioner was asked to work on Tammy. The Persian was totally co-operative, at first lying flattened on her belly and then allowing herself to be turned over onto her back, remaining immobile with her legs in the air, 'like a stuffed toy'. The major area of body stress was in the neck. A few hours after the releases, Tammy started eating again. Within a short time she was once again a healthy, rounded feline. It appears that the tension in the neck was irritating the spinal nerves to the extent that the muscles of the throat were constricted, preventing the cat from swallowing. One presumes that she must have jerked her neck in a misjudged jump or a fall.

A passion for penguins

This event took place some years ago, in the early days of the penguin colony at Boulders Beach near Simon's Town in the Cape. A BSR practitioner took frequent walks on the beach and noticed that a female penguin was struggling to move around, and stayed close to a particular large rock. Her mate was very protective and became aggressive if approached. Over several days the female remained under the shelter of the rock. The practitioner could not resist trying to

help, so she enlisted the assistance of her husband and together they waited for the male penguin to go fishing.

They dragged the female out from under the rock, and while her husband held the animal down, she proceeded to carry out BSR. Although she was only vaguely familiar with penguin structure, having cleaned and fed oil-soaked penguins in the past, she knew she could do no harm with the releases, and there was a chance that she may do some good. While she worked the penguin bellowed in protest, and she hoped no one would call the SPCA to report a case of cruelty. Several days later she was overjoyed to see the result of her ministrations – the female penguin was walking again, although a bit unsteadily, and going down to the water with the male. She decided not to schedule a follow-up appointment.

A windy dog

Chutney, an eighteen-month-old Staffordshire bull terrier, had an exuberant personality, and was the ideal companion for his young owners, except for one unfortunate characteristic – he had continuous flatulence. The couple told the BSR practitioner that the problem began the day after Chutney nearly hanged himself.

On an outing in their pick-up truck, the dog was riding in the open back, his lead tied to the tailgate of the vehicle. When they arrived at the beach, he was so excited that he leaped off the truck. He remained hanging in the air with his collar pulled tight around his neck until his owners rescued him.

The practitioner noted that there was such intense body stress in Chutney's neck that it had lost its normal curve. After two sessions the neck stabilised, and the flatulence abruptly ceased. How may this be explained? The neck tension must have been causing pressure on certain nerves of the autonomic nervous system, affecting connections to the digestive system. Some disturbance of normal function had

occurred, such as excessive secretion of gastric acid, resulting in production of gas.

Chutney's owners were advised to safeguard their dog's neck by using a harness lead, which fastens around the chest, rather than a collar lead.

A lame horse

June acquired a horse which, she believed, had been neglected and abused by his previous owners. The animal had a lame front leg. She asked her BSR practitioner to see if she could help, but warned her that this was an aggressive horse, prone to biting. While June distracted the horse by feeding him sugar lumps, the practitioner stood on a stool and released tension throughout the neck. The horse was walking normally a few days later.

Animal intuition

Animals are usually very receptive to BSR, and seem to have an instinctive knowing that the practitioner's actions are aimed at helping them. Many BSR practitioners have had the experience of a dog coming over to them and positioning its lower back or neck under their hands, 'asking' for its stress to be released. It appears that the animal's intuition tells it that this is a person who has something of benefit to offer it.

When do you need BSR?

Initially three appointments are made for a new client, the second one usually three days after the first, and the third several days later. This allows the body to go through the process of releasing stress – it undergoes changes and adaptations after each session. The practitioner advises the client when to return, based on what has been observed.

It may be necessary for the client to have a follow-up session within a few days, if there is rapid releasing of deep 'layers' of tension.

In other cases a longer interval between sessions may be indicated – possibly a week or two, or a month – to allow time for even deeper stored tension to be accessed and released.

How long will the process take?

Everyone would like a 'quick fix' to their health problems. However, each case is different and the body has its own timing. Obviously a recent event of body stress may be resolved quickly, while in a long-term condition the changes may be slower and more gradual. The BSR practitioner can give a client a sense of the progress being made, by observing certain signs of response to the releases.

Forty years of headaches

As an architect of fifty-three, Gerard's work pressure was aggravated by having to cope with intense headaches which occurred without fail every two to three weeks. This had been the pattern of his life for forty years, ever since a fall from a climbing apparatus in the school gym. Over this time he had tried 'every treatment and cure you could think of', some for a long period.

When body stress was released in his spine, immediately the headache frequency changed – he had headaches every few days, which he called 'light'. But once a month the severe kind returned, and he had to spend the day lying down in the dark. Painkillers gave no relief. Gerard was not happy – he said he now had his 'well-known severe friend every four weeks, and the lighter ones as a new regular companion'.

He had a monthly BSR session, and this situation continued for seven months. 'How much longer do I need to come?' he asked, beginning to despair. The practitioner felt convinced that BSR would help if she could persuade him to increase the frequency of the

sessions. So she made him an offer he could not refuse. 'From now on I'll take no payment until your headaches are gone for three months, however long it takes. When that is achieved, you'll pay me half of the normal fee for all the preceding sessions.'

Gerard accepted the offer with pleasure, encouraged by the faith the practitioner had in her work. So a new pattern began. He went every week for six weeks, and had only one severe headache. When there was no recurrence for three weeks, his appointments were reduced to once a fortnight. In week eleven he felt some heaviness in his head, in weeks thirteen and fifteen a minor headache. Then – success – no headache at all for four months. He was very happy to pay up as agreed.

He is now on a monthly schedule for maintenance. In the past year, he had only one major headache and one minor. It is now two-and-a-half years since he started with BSR. Why did the process unfold in this way? During those forty years, the tension from the fall was stored in his neck and back, and his body adapted to deal with it. However, with the nature of his work as an architect, working for hours at a drawing board, the pressure would build up every few weeks to the point that the surface muscles would tighten and cause intense further irritation to the nervous system. The BSR process gradually unlocked the layers of compression.

Giving up too soon

It is understandable that when people have had pain and limitation for a long time, they are hoping for fast relief, and may become despondent when this does not happen. Each case is different and a practitioner cannot accurately predict how many BSR sessions a person may require. However, the changes that are occurring, some obvious, others subtle, show how the body is responding and progressing in its process of releasing the stored tension, and this gives some indication of when the next appointment should be booked.

Anne, a woman in her forties, felt no relief from her lower-back and leg pain after her first BSR session, so she cancelled her two further appointments.

A month later, at the hairdresser, she started talking about her problems to the woman in the chair beside her. 'What you need is Body Stress Release,' her neighbour exclaimed. 'Oh no,' said Anne, 'I tried that and it didn't work.' When she admitted that she had only had one session the enthusiastic client gave her a long lecture on BSR being a logical process, and not a 'panel-beating quick fix'.

Anne was convinced and returned to our practice to tell this story. 'This time,' she said, 'I'll see the process through and follow all your advice.' Happily, several sessions later she was free of pain.

BSR practitioners feel it is important to inform our clients about our findings, and educate them as to how BSR works. Armed with understanding, they are more likely to persist until they 'turn the corner' and allow the self-healing mechanisms to be activated.

Gradual progress over a long period

In some cases of long-term body stress the improvement may be slow. Releasing the stored tension is like peeling away the layers of an onion, to reach and release the original core injury.

Aletta, a businesswoman of forty-six, had a long history of trauma, which included head injuries from a car accident as a child and a bad fall in her twenties. As a result of herniated discs in her lower back she had undergone a fusion of four vertebrae, secured by titanium plates and screws. She was now experiencing generalised muscular aches and such intense pain in her right leg that she could not straighten it. She had been diagnosed with fibromyalgia and ME, and felt despondent as she could no longer do any form of exercise.

Her BSR practitioner describes Aletta as being grey with pain at her first appointment, and she had to work extremely lightly, releasing body stress throughout the spine, avoiding the area of the surgery. After the first session Aletta slept well. However, over the next four appointments the sciatic pain became more severe. After five weeks the leg pain was coming and going, and she had started feeling pain below her ribs at night.

Seventeen sessions and five months later, Aletta's lower back started aching, as well as her 'good' leg. There were spasms in her shoulder-blade area and her right arm was stiff. However, she did not consider giving up, as she understood that her body was going through necessary changes to undo the trauma of the past. The pain ranged from extreme to bearable, and she said, 'I have a life again.'

About a year after her first session, she started crying during the releases. She explained that these were tears of gratitude, as she had never again experienced the intensity of pain that she had before BSR, and it was wonderful to know how it feels to be pain-free. She now goes to the gym and does sailing, and at times still feels varying degrees of pain. She never misses her monthly BSR maintenance session.

The 'one-shot' miracles

It may occur that BSR catalyses a very fast healing process which appears to defy logic. A man in his sixties, heavily overweight, was reluctant to try BSR, and only came to our practice because his wife insisted. He had been experiencing back and leg pain for years, had 'tried everything' and had no hope of anything helping his situation.

When he returned for his second appointment, he was radiant with enthusiasm, as all his pain was gone. In view of his history, I expected the usual process of 'layers of tension' letting go over a period, so I cautioned him that there would very likely be a coming and going of pain over the next few weeks.

However, the unexpected happened — no return of pain. I suggested a follow-up appointment in one week, then two weeks, then a month,

constantly expecting a deeper level of body stress to manifest. But at each session only minimal residual tension could be detected. A year later, the client sent us a letter to say how grateful he was that he was still pain-free.

This illustrates the fact that each case is individual, with its own wisdom and timing.

The return of symptoms

Does the return of symptoms mean that BSR has not been effective? When a person has had a long-term condition of body stress, originating from an incident in the distant past, there is an accumulation of layers of muscle tension. After several sessions of BSR there may be total relief from pain or other symptoms. As time passes, possibly for days, weeks or even months, the body continues unlocking deeper levels of stored tension. As the muscles relax back to normal tone, there may be an uncovering of the original cause. The return of pain or stiffness means that the body is ready to deal with this, with further help from BSR. Therefore one should not become despondent about a problem which appears to return – it is an indication that more stored tension needs to be attended to.

Going beyond healing to prevention

Most people who seek BSR care are looking for relief from pain, stiffness or other discomfort or malfunction. However, BSR has a broader objective – it is concerned with assisting the body in maintaining health.

To promote efficiency of body function we need to keep ourselves free from stored tension. To prevent body stress from accumulating it makes sense to be assessed several times a year, before problems arise.

When there is relief from a long-term serious condition, a person is usually highly motivated to take action to prevent the problem returning.

Reinette, who is in her sixties, spent twelve months visiting numerous specialists. She had an MRI scan and was also treated by various types of alternative and complementary practitioners. There was no change or improvement in her problem – extreme sciatic pain, with almost constant cramping in the right calf, and pins and needles that 'ran up and down' her leg. BSR was her last attempt to regain some mobility and pain relief. She literally hopped into the practice, as she could hardly lift her right leg.

Her whole lower back was hypersensitive and the practitioner had to work very lightly. Contrary to expectations, Reinette was walking normally when she came for her second appointment. She reported that the leg pain had worsened the day after the session, and then had virtually disappeared. There was no more cramping, and the pins and needles only occurred after sitting for long periods of time. Her left hip joint had started aching, but that cleared up after the third session.

Reinette realised that she had been overstressing her lower back when doing housework and caring for her grandchildren. She was now very careful in the way she bent to lift the children, and avoided twisting when sweeping. She has learned to listen to her body, and does not wait until she is in pain – if her lower back begins to feel stiff for longer than a few days she goes for a BSR maintenance session.

> Most people honour the principle of prevention when it comes to their car, ensuring that it is serviced regularly. We would be wise to give our bodies the same consideration.

CHAPTER 13

Body Stress Release for babies and children

Has your child been labelled as naughty, disruptive, a dreamer or a slow learner? In this chapter you will read about screaming babies, toddlers with growing pains, mysterious night attacks, bed-wetting, attention problems, and brain-damaged children. It has been found that so many situations that blight children's lives may be the result of stored tension.

When we see the dramatic changes in children after their body stress is released, we have the sense that their future is being transformed. Their lives can be directed along a path of healthy development, instead of being derailed into dysfunction and lost potential.

The youngest person Ewald and I have attended to was a two-day-old baby girl. It had been a difficult first birth for the mother – the parents were concerned as the baby could not suckle properly; her tongue kept flicking to the corner of her mouth. Body stress was released in her neck and by the following day she was suckling normally.

The birth process is stressful for a baby, and may cause tension to become locked into the neck and lower back. The procedures carried out in a Caesarean birth may also result in body stress. It is very likely that babies experience some degree of shock, being thrust suddenly into an alien outside world, after the months of floating in the sanctuary of the mother's body.

A two-month-old baby was born with the umbilical cord caught around his neck. He cried almost constantly, and always vomited after feeding. After three BSR sessions in which neck stress was released, the vomiting ceased and the crying was much reduced; he was sleeping better, and starting to put on weight.

A baby may continue to store emotional shock that has occurred at birth. A girl of twenty months vomited every time she had a fright, even a small one like tripping. She also woke every night and demanded a bottle. Her mother mentioned that she was terrified of doctors and nurses, or anyone wearing a white uniform. Tension was released in her neck and lower back. After three sessions she was sleeping through the night, and no longer vomited if startled.

Signs of body stress in babies

A baby that has pain or discomfort may cry almost constantly. 'Screamers' are often seen at BSR practices. If medical conditions have been ruled out and the baby is feeding normally and is obviously not hungry, it is likely that the baby has body stress.

When the neck is stressed, the baby appears restless, and keeps moving the head and arms, even when sleeping. If there is tension in the lower back, the baby may squirm and cry when his hips are lifted during a nappy change. There may be constipation or diarrhoea.

Screaming

Neck stress from forceps delivery

I will never forget Andrew, who had a difficult birth, a forceps delivery. His face was screwed up into a mask of agony, and the screams he emitted were incongruously loud for such a small body.

'It has been six months of hell,' said his young mother, Carol. 'The only time he stops screaming is if I sway him very slowly.' As she did this, the screaming decreased to crying. 'I can't put him down at all, until he's so exhausted he falls asleep – and then he wakes up after an hour and starts yelling immediately.'

She was close to tears. 'I can't stand it much longer. I'm worn out, and the strain on my marriage is awful.' She said that medical tests had not revealed any problems, and he was able to feed adequately. Carol's voice was tremulous. 'If there's nothing wrong with him, then it must be me – I must be doing something wrong.'

When I placed him on his stomach, Andrew stiffened his arms, arching his body backwards. He twisted his head from side to side. I touched his neck very lightly and he hunched his shoulders and bellowed. It was a struggle to reach the contact points on his neck, as he resisted with all his might. The patterns of body stress were similar to those seen after a whiplash in a car accident. Then, as the last stressed site was released, to his mother's astonishment he fell instantly into a deep sleep.

At the next session three days later Carol reported that Andrew had slept for ten hours. He was still crying constantly, but she described it as sounding more normal. His neck remained very sensitive to touch, but the BSR checks showed reduced tension.

Three days later Andrew's return was announced by ear-splitting yells. 'This only started yesterday,' said Carol. 'For two days it was amazing – he stopped crying completely and slept for hours.'

The BSR tests showed intense body stress in the lower neck. The surface muscles had relaxed, uncovering a deeper level of stress which had not yet been dealt with. The baby tensed with pain as the gentle releasing pressure was applied. I warned Carol that he may have an uncomfortable day or two, as feeling would be restored to nerves now that the deeper stress had been unlocked. It would take a while for any inflammation and sensitivity to withdraw.

The young woman who returned the following week looked transformed, her face relaxed, eyes shining. She held out a sleeping baby. 'I have a totally different child. For the past two days he hasn't cried, except when he was wet. And the wonderful thing is – for the first time he responds to me when I smile or show him something.'

Andrew woke up just then and looked around the room with a calm curiosity. He did not arch his body when placed on his stomach. There was only some minor residual stress in his neck to be dealt with and he was completely co-operative.

A year later, it was gratifying to hear from Carol that there had been no recurrence of Andrew's problems. She was enjoying motherhood so much she had decided to have another baby.

Defective muscle tone

Nerve hyper-activity

A seven-month-old baby was diagnosed as having 'high muscle tone'. Her body appeared rigid, and she could not bend or sit. Body stress was released throughout the spine. As the practitioner handed the baby back to her mother, the little body instantly relaxed into a sitting position. In this case the pressure on the spinal nerves had caused the transmission to be overactive.

Nerve hypo-activity

Delia had been born by Caesarian section, and at first seemed normal. But she never learned to crawl or talk, she was constantly constipated and became extremely obese. By the age of two-and-a-half she resembled a 'blimp' lying on the floor. She could only raise her head slightly, and her mobility was limited to a slithering manoeuvre. She frequently uttered high-pitched screams, apparently out of frustration at being unable to communicate.

The diagnosis was 'excessive hypotonia' – severe muscle weakness, but no cause could be found for this condition. When her mother took her to a BSR practitioner, she expressed her shame and sorrow at seeing her child in this helpless state, while other children of that age were running around and playing.

The practitioner's assessment of Delia showed widespread body stress. The neck in particular 'felt like a rock'. At first this appears contradictory to the diagnosis of low muscle tone, but it is in fact quite logical. The compression around the spinal nerves had caused the muscles close to the spine to be contracted. This pressure was also having the effect of distorting the transmission of nerve impulses to the muscles of the limbs, neck and trunk, causing under-activity of muscle fibres, hence the lack of tone.

Once the body stress was released there was a rapid improvement in communication to the muscles. After the second session, Delia amazed her mother by grabbing onto a low table and pulling herself into a standing position. After eight sessions she could walk if her mother held her hands. In addition, she was no longer constipated, and had lost a great deal of her excess fat. She was able to crawl, although her movements were not yet co-ordinated. There were no more screaming tantrums, as she had started to say her first words.

Colic

A baby with colic may cause its parents to despair, feeling undermined by exhaustion and totally helpless. A colicky baby may scream for hours, pulling up its legs and clenching its fists, or it may stiffen its legs and arch its back. It usually begins at about three weeks and ceases by four months. It is believed to be a cramping in the intestines due to the baby swallowing air while feeding. Often the baby may regurgitate milk. As the cause is not clear, it may be blamed on the anxiety of the mother being transferred to the baby.

From the BSR point of view, there appears to be a logical explanation, and many babies with colic have been helped. The major sites of body stress are found in the lower spine, probably caused by the birth process. Initially the baby's body deals with this by tightening the long muscles of the back in a splinting action. This causes the abdominal muscles at the front of the body to lock up in compensation, which refers tension into the diaphragm. The tension in the diaphragm causes irritation to the oesophagus which passes through it, resulting in excess stomach acidity and pain.

As weeks or months pass, if nothing is done to relieve the muscle tension, the shorter, deeper muscles of the back begin to tighten into a defensive state. This allows the more superficial muscles and diaphragm to relax, and the colic goes away.

However, the stress in the deep back muscles leads to compression of the spinal nerves of the lower back. These nerves supply both the intestinal area and legs, so in time the baby may start to have irregular bowel movements, even constipation or diarrhoea. Later when starting to walk, the child may complain of sore legs – so-called 'growing pains'.

The BSR approach is to release the lower-back compression and the diaphragm spasm, thereby relieving the tension on the oesophagus and the irritation of the nerves supplying the digestive system. In addition, possible problems that may develop later from the impact on the nervous system are avoided.

Could stored stress contribute to cot death?

Sudden infant death syndrome (SIDS), or cot death, is the unexplained death of an apparently healthy baby, usually between the ages of two and four months. No cause is found even on detailed medical investigation.

A young couple in France came close to experiencing this tragedy. One morning their three-month-old baby boy, Justin, gave three loud shrieks. The parents rushed into his room, and found the baby had stopped breathing and was turning blue. In panic the mother picked him up and shook him and he took a gasp of air. The baby was rushed to the hospital where the doctor pronounced him perfectly well.

A week later this terrifying event was repeated, this time preceded by two sharp yells from Justin. Once again the doctors detected no problems. The parents now lived in dread. They kept the cot beside their bed, and while one slept the other watched over the baby. Throughout the day the mother kept him beside her.

A few days later Justin again stopped breathing, after giving one scream. The doctors were baffled. Every test that was carried out – scans, blood and urine analysis – showed nothing unusual.

The baby's grandmother, who lives in Holland, told the parents about a BSR practitioner who has helped many babies with various problems. With no other option available, the family flew to Holland. The practitioner was fully booked for weeks ahead, but she assessed Justin during her lunch break. The baby shrieked while body stress was released in his neck and lower back. Three days later he again complained loudly as the procedure was carried out. On the third and final appointment, as the practitioner placed Justin on his mother's chest, she bent towards him and said, 'Aren't you happy that you met me?' She was amazed when he looked into her face and laughed out loud. Both the mother and father cried tears of relief and joy. This time Justin showed no pain reaction and lay quietly as the releases were done.

The young parents returned to France with a sense that they could relax and trust in life again. They reported that Justin was very different – happy and relaxed. Before the releases, they had not realised that he

was not a contented baby. He had displayed many signs of irritability and discomfort which, as new parents, they had assumed were normal. Two months later the family flew back to Holland so that the young mother could have three BSR sessions, to help her recover from the extreme stress she had undergone. Justin had a 'maintenance' BSR check. Six months later his grandmother reported that he was thriving.

How can Justin's case be explained? Even though his birth had been trouble-free, tension had become locked into his spine. It is possible that the compression in the neck was disturbing transmission in the specific spinal nerves (cervical nerves three, four and five) which give rise to the phrenic nerves. These two nerves cause the regular contractions of the diaphragm during breathing. At times, when the baby moved his head in a way that aggravated the nerve irritation, it not only caused pain that made him cry out, but was intense enough to disrupt the nerve impulses to the diaphragm, and breathing stopped.

How are babies assessed for body stress?

The BSR practitioner carries out the checks and releases while the baby is lying on the mother's chest. If the baby is older, he may feel more at ease lying across the mother's lap.

The pressure applied in the releases is very gentle and quite often the baby falls asleep immediately after the process is completed.

Babies usually respond very quickly to BSR, as the stress has not been stored in the body for a long time – there are usually no 'layers' of tension locked in.

It is advisable to have a baby assessed for body stress within a few months of birth, even if there do not appear to be any problems. In this way, if there is any tension present, it will be released before it builds up to have an adverse impact on the nervous system, with consequences later in life.

Because of the intense bond between a baby and a mother, it is very beneficial to the baby for the mother to be free of stored stress, so mothers are advised to be assessed for body stress along with their babies.

Toddlers

Small children are likely to accumulate body stress as a result of frequent falls or jerks while playing, or from trying to lift heavy objects. They cannot easily verbalise what they are feeling, but the parents may observe signs indicating the presence of stored tension. For example, a normally good-natured child will become sullen or irritable. One mother who brought her little boy for BSR every few months would say, 'I know it's time – my little angel is turning into a monster.'

'Growing pains'

A toddler may constantly demand to be picked up and carried, and complain of 'sore legs'. In BSR we find that so-called 'growing pains' result from lower-back body stress, with pressure irritating the nerves supplying the legs. Growing is a normal process. If it caused pain, all children would experience it.

'Sore tummy'

On several occasions a four-year-old girl awoke screaming, not long after falling asleep. She held her abdomen and cried, 'Sore tummy!'. Her parents rushed her to hospital, but each time no medical cause was found. It was a frightening situation – her parents dreaded the next time this mysterious condition would occur, resulting in the frantic night-time dash to the hospital.

In the BSR consultation, lower-back and diaphragm stress were found. On questioning the mother a logical explanation emerged. Occasionally, before going to bed, the little girl requested a drink of iced fruit juice. The cold acidic liquid aggravated the tension in the diaphragm, causing it to spasm painfully. The mother stopped giving her the iced drinks and there were no more panicked flights to the hospital.

In less intense cases, a small child with diaphragm stress may talk about a 'funny feeling in my tummy'.

Constipation

A girl of four had a bowel movement only every four days, before which she would go purple in the face and roll on the floor with pain. As there was no medical explanation for the problem, a psychological assessment had been suggested. The parents decided to try BSR first. The child had a dramatic reaction to the first session, in which body stress in the lower spine was released – she vomited throughout the night. Then, over the next two weeks, she experienced a bowel movement every second day. In considering the possible cause of the intense body stress, the parents said the little girl had not had any major falls. However, when she was a baby, they used to throw her up in the air in big swinging motions.

Constipation, bloating and gas

Constant constipation, bloating and gas were problems that plagued a boy of twenty months almost all of his short life. He was pasty-faced and very restless. His parents had 'tried everything', even resorting to anal stretching twice, but nothing had helped. Within a day of having body stress released in his lower back, the boy had a good bowel movement. After three sessions the parents exclaimed, 'Wonderful! He is really fine.'

At a follow-up visit six weeks later they said it was 'a miracle' as there was no recurrence of the condition.

Bed-wetting

A three-year-old girl was described by her father as naughty, as medical tests had shown no reason for her continual bed-wetting. After three BSR sessions during which tension was released from the lower back, the bouts of bed-wetting decreased in frequency, and a week later ceased entirely.

Assessing toddlers for body stress

At first a small child may be nervous, not knowing what to expect, and wary that something painful might be done.

It is more reassuring to the child to be seated on the mother's lap, with the practitioner applying gentle pressure on the arms and legs to demonstrate how BSR feels. Then the child is usually willing to lie across the mother's lap so that the pressure tests and releases can be carried out.

In a later session the child may agree to lie on the BSR couch. I once lowered a teddy bear on the couch, wiggled its feet, and prodded its entire back in simulated releases. Its owner, a suspicious four-year-old, decided that if it was all right for Teddy, it would be fine for him, and he willingly climbed onto the couch.

As BSR is a gentle procedure, even nervous children become trusting and co-operative.

Small children who have experienced BSR develop a remarkable awareness of their bodies. Several have commented that after the releases they feel 'lighter'. A three-year-old boy, who had regular BSR since birth, was able to feel when his body was becoming uncomfortable. We were amused to hear that he would tell his mother, 'I need a Meggersee!'

The wisdom of a four-year-old

Dale's story illustrates how conscious children are of their body and its needs. This four-year-old boy suffered from stomach ache, especially after eating. At times it was so severe that he was reluctant to eat, knowing it would increase his pain. He had great difficulty in going to the toilet. His mother was dismayed to see her happy, sensitive and caring child becoming more and more aggressive.

She could think of two possible causes of his problems – his birth had been difficult and drawn-out, and at one year old he had fallen off a couch onto his head. After that event he had often been constipated, and usually cried during feeding.

Dale seemed withdrawn at his first BSR session, but he showed the practitioner where his 'tummy ache' was. Three days later, at the second session, his mother happily described what had happened – each day

he had an enormous bowel movement, and his mood was more relaxed and open. The boy, however, showed he had no time to chat, as he went straight to the BSR couch and stood waiting impatiently to be checked and released.

At the third visit, Dale gave the practitioner a beaming smile when he arrived, and again went straight to the couch. His mother reported that he was going to the toilet without any pain, and his behaviour was transforming – he was more friendly to other children.

This time, as Dale stepped off the couch, he looked at the practitioner with a radiant expression. 'Now I'm finished!' he declared. She made a follow-up appointment for Dale in six weeks' time, in case there was an uncovering of a deeper level of body stress.

When that day came, the practitioner found only the mother sitting in the waiting room, but she had a message from Dale. 'Tell the lady that I don't need to come back – my tummy is fine! But you go, Mummy, because it's good for your back!' She said that Dale now whistles and sings when he goes to the toilet, and this is music to her ears.

Older children

Children may sit incorrectly, for example reading or studying hunched over on a bed. This may induce body stress in the neck and lower back.

Often teenagers watch television half-lying, slumped on a couch. This reverses the normal lumbar curve and will cause pressure to build up in the spine.

These days the emotional demands on teenagers are immense – achievement at school, peer pressure to measure up, hormonal surges. At this time a child's budding self-esteem may be easily eroded. As they approach puberty, children become more self-conscious, and may develop poor posture. Hunched shoulders, a contracted chest, and a downward-tilted head occur as a defensive mechanism against the new challenges and stresses of the teenage years. Muscles tighten and tension becomes locked into the body.

Learning difficulties

A child with tension in the neck may lack concentration, and thus perform poorly at school. With body stress in the lower back, the child may be restless, constantly moving to ease the discomfort, and will be labelled inattentive and disruptive.

At ten, Diane was the class troublemaker. She refused to sit still, and constantly disturbed the other children. Her marks were poor and her teacher assumed she was not very bright. The BSR assessment detected body stress in the lower-, mid-back and neck areas. Her parents were surprised, as Diane never complained of any discomfort or pain, and she was very active, if not over-active. After several sessions, the BSR tests showed stability. Some months later, her mother reported that Diane's marks had soared, and her delighted teacher had asked, 'What on earth have you done to this child?' Her behaviour had become calm and co-operative, and she was able to concentrate.

In Diane's case, the body stress was causing a constant sense of irritation and unease, so that she felt distracted all the time. She could not verbalise this, as to her this was a normal state of being. Her parents theorised that her problems may have been caused by a fall down a flight of stairs when she was five.

Personality changes

From introvert to extrovert

The mother of a nine-year-old boy said he had become introverted and withdrawn ever since a freak accident three years before. He had run into a rope suspended between two poles – it caught him across the neck and jerked his head backwards. After three sessions of BSR she was overjoyed to tell us that she had her 'sunny-natured' child back. No doubt the effort to suppress the pain in his neck and upper back had undermined his energy and spirit.

The boy who hated school

Six-year-old Ben hated school because he had to sit all day, which was boring compared to running around and playing. His father said he fell frequently, his small movements were rather unco-ordinated, and he could not keep still for five minutes. The teachers thought he may have dyslexia, and he was a slow learner. Also, although he was a lively boy, he tired very easily.

In his first BSR session he squirmed and writhed on the couch, and could not lie for long. But by the third time he was completely relaxed during the releasing process. After three further sessions spread out over the next four months, a transformation had taken place. He confided in his practitioner that he did not hate school any more – in fact it was even interesting sometimes, and he liked going there. He did not mind having to sit still.

Ben's father said that besides his improvement in school and his increased stamina, there had been another interesting change. The boy had always had a fear of heights, and would not climb onto anything higher than a metre. On taking him to an amusement park, the father was amazed to see Ben was eager to go on the rides and climb up a jungle gym. The practitioner explained the logic of this: while tension was causing compression to the spinal nerves supplying the legs, Ben instinctively knew he did not have full control of his legs, and could easily fall from a height. Now that he had normal awareness of his limbs, there was no reason to be afraid.

On reviewing this case, she says, 'A few BSR sessions have helped this little boy to have a normal life in school. He has been spared from having to undergo psychological and retraining programmes, and the stigma of being an awkward or difficult child. I don't know who was more happy after all: the boy, the father or me!'

Nightmares

Duncan, aged six, was a healthy, lively, intelligent and well-behaved child. Suddenly he began waking every night with dreadful nightmares. When this continued for two weeks, his parents thought the source of the problem may be something happening at his pre-school. When they approached the teacher, she suggested they take Duncan to BSR.

Quite intense pressure was found and released throughout his neck and lower back. That night the boy slept right through, undisturbed, and since then there have been no more nightmares. It is a mystery to his parents what had caused the body stress. Of course, little boys can be very adventurous, and may have falls they keep from their parents – especially if they happened in a forbidden activity or place.

Avoidance of medication

Matthew's school advised his parents to speak to their doctor about putting him on Ritalin, as his behaviour was disturbing the other children. He was seven years old, and could not sit still or concentrate; he was clumsy and frequently fell off his chair. There were several other significant problems: since birth he had been making noises at night and sleepwalking, and he complained about his sore legs. All of this suggested neck and lower-back compression, which would be keeping him in an agitated state, as though he could not feel at home in his body. His history backed this up – he had been born by emergency Caesarian section because the cord was wrapped around his neck, and as a baby he had been constipated.

Immediately after the releases, Matthew's leg pain ceased. He had a set-back the next day when the children at school knocked him over, and he fell and hit his head. His neck went into a spasm, pulling towards his shoulder. After six BSR sessions, the sleepwalking and night noises stopped. Since then, his mother has been able to take him shopping with her – instead of flinging items off the supermarket shelves, he stays at her side, calm and contented.

How did the release of body stress have a calming effect on the behaviour of Duncan and Matthew? A possible explanation is that the stored tension had been causing ongoing irritation to nerve pathways of the sympathetic nervous system, triggering a 'fight or flight' mode. The boys' bodies had been geared up to respond to threats which did not exist.

Bed-wetting in a teenager

One can imagine the shame of a fifteen-year-old who had to hide the secret of being a bed-wetter. He was unable to sleep over at a friend's house or go on overnight camping trips. Over five BSR sessions, 'layers' of tension released from his lower back. The bed-wetting abruptly ceased. His mother said his self-confidence had rocketed and he had become far more outgoing. A year later he fell heavily in a rugby tackle, and once again he lost bladder control while he was sleeping. He returned for two sessions of BSR, and the problem resolved itself.

Brain-damaged children

Many BSR practitioners have worked with children who have been born with some form of brain damage or abnormality. The parents have turned to BSR as a last resort. Practitioners have been privileged to witness BSR being the catalyst for some minor and major 'miracles'. In some cases small changes have upgraded a child's limited life expression. In others there have been dramatic transformations.

A six-year-old brain-damaged boy had both arms and legs bent in constant spasm. His mobility was limited to rolling around on the floor. His parents had taken him to the USA to learn how to do 'patterning' with him. Every day volunteers came to help with this work – manually unbending and stretching his limbs for hours. These manoeuvres were aimed at stimulating brain centres to unlock the muscular spasm.

It was difficult to do the BSR checks on him, but he responded dynamically to the releases which were carried out on his spine. After three sessions his arms and legs relaxed and straightened and for the first time in his life he was able to crawl. He soon learned to pull himself up holding onto furniture and started walking. Two weeks later his walking led to running. It was a great joy for his parents to see their child set free

from a state that had isolated him from his surroundings. His experience of the world expanded enormously, and he was able to interact with other people. Sadly, he did not develop the ability to speak, but he could communicate with gestures and sounds.

A three-year-old girl had both arms contracted against her chest and she did not speak. At the first BSR session, as the practitioner was turning her onto her back, having completed the releases on the spine, the little girl reached out with one arm. The parents' excitement escalated as over the next few weeks of BSR the child's arms became flexible. The supreme moment came when one day she spontaneously spoke her first words.

Jake's story is even more dramatic. His mother noticed that the baby was not using the right side of his body, so she took him to a paediatrician. An extensive examination included a brain scan, and the parents were faced with a chilling revelation – the left side of the brain (which controls the right side of the body) was extremely underdeveloped. The diagnosis was hemiplegia – paralysis of one side of the body, and they were told the child would never walk or talk.

When Jake was about ten months old his mother took him to a BSR practitioner because of his constipation. Over several months, she brought him back whenever the constipation started recurring. One day she noticed that he was trying to grab his paralysed leg with his left arm. Then he started moving that leg, crawling, and even standing for a few seconds. The parents' excitement mounted when Jake took a few steps. The progress continued steadily over the next four years, with regular BSR, and he began talking, and then walking on his own. Greater movement developed in the fingers.

The day arrived when the little boy came running into the practice and gave the practitioner a hug radiating love – a very emotional moment. Jake now attends a 'normal' school, and his only limitation appears to be some lack of fine movement in the hand.

How can BSR have an impact on the brain? We assume that as the stored tension and compression are released from the spinal nerves, the sensory nerves of the spinal cord are stimulated. The reticular activating system in the brain stem receives sufficient prompting to forward the impulses to the cerebral cortex. Thus the relaying of information to the brain is enhanced. The messages then travel from the sensory centres of the brain to the motor areas. In certain cases this apparently has the effect of activating some functions to 'wake up' and be restored, such as the motor supply to the muscles of the limbs, and connections to the speech centre in the brain.

Regular BSR for children

Parents are advised to take their children to be checked at regular intervals, to prevent body stress from accumulating. By keeping the communication system free from disturbance the body is assisted in ensuring that the child's growth and development are normal and healthy.

Also, problems that arise in later life, such as back pain and headaches, or degenerative conditions like osteoarthritis, may be traced back to trauma in childhood – falls and sports injuries. If the body stress is not dealt with, it initiates a process of degeneration.

The effect of shock

Besides the future physical consequences of a childhood injury, shock may have an impact on the child's psychological well-being. As tension locks into structures of the body, the shock of the event also becomes stored, undermining and distorting the emotional development of the child.

At the age of thirty-four, Evan's stiff lower back and an ache in one thigh led him to BSR. After a number of sessions, the pain was gone from his leg, but his lower spine suddenly became so painful he could not sit for long, and he could hardly turn his upper body. The release of compression from the spinal nerves, resulting in the return of

suppressed sensation, was accompanied by a dramatic restoration of normal function – he could urinate without pain. For his whole life urination had always been accompanied by a burning sensation.

At his next session he underwent a startling experience. A strange sensation of numbness crept over his body, and tears started flowing. He felt no sadness and yet the tears continued. Then a long-buried memory surfaced – he saw himself at eight years old, falling off a roof, and then his father running, carrying him.

A few days later the pain subsided in his back, and a general sense of well-being filled him. When asked how he thought the stored shock had undermined him, he said that his whole life he had suffered from a sense of inadequacy, of not being good enough.

After any childhood accident it is possible that the memory of the incident will remain stored in the body. Even if the child does not appear to be physically injured, it could make an enormous difference to his or her future emotional well-being to have the body stress released.

A child's point of view

David, a very verbal three-year-old child, had complained of a sore back and legs, and he had three sessions of BSR. A few days later his mother, a BSR student, was rehearsing an introductory talk she would be giving in class. David suddenly interrupted. 'I can give a talk. I know what Body Stress Release is!'

His mother was amused and said, 'Okay – go ahead.'

This is what David said: 'Cuts and bruises get locked in your legs. The BSR practicker unlocks them with his fingers or with the key he keeps in his pocket. Then he throws them out the window and you jump up and dance around!'

CHAPTER 14

The chemical minefield

This subject has relevance to everyone as our environment has come to resemble a chemical minefield. Chemical stress may have a severe impact on many people, while the causes remain a mystery to them.

I feel that one of our most vital discoveries in BSR has been pinpointing the precise physical effects of chemically-induced body stress, and working out the specific techniques necessary to release it.

The discovery

The process of discovery began in the mid-eighties with Linda, a woman of about thirty-five, who was hospitalised for a headache that was so intense that she described it as a volcano erupting out of the top of her head. When medical tests came up negative and morphine did little to decrease the pain, she left the hospital and her husband brought her to us.

While she lay with her eyes screwed shut in agony, I carried out the normal pressure tests, while Ewald monitored her body's responses. None of the releases I applied helped. Finally, as I tested some unusual sites and directions in the neck, Ewald noted a strong reaction in the leg muscles. As soon as I performed this new release Linda gave a great gasp – the volcano pressure in her head deflated and all the pain faded away.

As we were discussing this miracle, searching for possible causes of this extreme body stress, she mentioned that she had eaten some sweet-melon just before the headache began. That proved to be a vital key. Over the next year we had many cases of 'chemical headaches' linked to certain fruits and vegetables, which the clients described as unusually large.

We met someone with connections in the agricultural sphere and he did some investigating. He discovered that at that time certain crops were being fed with a growth stimulator, which was absorbed into the flesh of the fruit or vegetable.

This information was confirmed by our cat Amica. She had a strange passion for sweet-melon – she smelled it the moment it was brought into the house, and would start meowing her demand for a slice. I gave her a piece of a suspiciously large melon, which she devoured and then immediately vomited up. After that if I offered her sweet-melon she would sniff at it and turn away. About six months later a client gave us a home-grown melon, small and chemical-free. I cut a slice for Amica – she smelled it, gave a 'rowr' of approval and ate it with delight.

We cautioned people to buy only normal-sized produce.

Chemical stress may also arise from insecticides sprayed on the fruit. To avoid the chemical impact, it is advisable to peel fruit unless you are sure it has been grown organically.

Signs of chemical stress

How do you know if you are suffering from chemically-induced body stress?

Usually, the effects come on suddenly – severe headache, often with a particular pattern of pain, e.g. on one side of the head, or through one eye into the forehead. Muscle tightness or pain is felt at the base of the skull, and in some cases there is dizziness or nausea. In addition, the person's face becomes very pale.

Over the years, in testing thousands of people, we found that chemical stress causes a particular pattern of body stress. In the upper neck the compression occurs at specific sites, with lines of tension always present in certain directions.

After the releases, usually the pain starts receding straight away, and colour floods back into the face.

In a few cases, we have found that if the level of the chemical is very high in the system, the neck stress will recur, possibly within hours or the next day. Further releases will have to be carried out, until the body has managed to reduce the substance to a concentration too low to induce body stress. It may help to drink a lot of water. It is advisable to avoid alcohol for the next day, so as not to add to the chemical load.

Low blood sugar

Do you ever have bouts of shakiness or shivering, nausea and dizziness, accompanied by a throbbing headache? Besides the physical sensations, you may also feel depressed and angry, even antisocial. These are signs of hypoglycaemia, or low blood sugar, which most people experience in a mild form when they either do not eat when hungry or if their diet is poor. Certain people are very susceptible to this condition. If they overload on sugar, or substitute food with coffee or alcohol, the body reacts by producing insulin, which causes the blood sugar level to drop dramatically.

This constitutes a form of chemical stress, and in such a case the BSR tests always reveal the typical chemical stress patterns in the neck area. It is essential for the person to start eating a normal diet as well as having the stored stress released.

Detective work: find the substance

As long as a person is exposed to a chemical to which he or she is sensitive, the chemical body stress will keep recurring. One needs to work out what the substance is, and exclude it. It may be something consumed, inhaled or absorbed through the skin – think back to when the headaches began.

A young woman realised that her problems dated back six months, to when she started using a new face cream. After BSR, she was advised to

stop using it and the headaches did not return. In some cases we have tracked the cause to a herbal skin cream. If something is labelled as natural, it does not mean it is 'innocent', as a person may have a sensitivity to that herb.

Mysterious cases

For several weeks I was attacked by a Wednesday headache, at about eleven in the morning. I started feeling dizzy and nauseous, with a squeezing sensation at the base of my skull. The pain burned a jagged path through my left ear and eye, culminating in an explosive throbbing in my forehead. Each time Ewald would detect the specific stress pattern that we find with chemical stress. After the neck and head releases the pain withdrew within minutes. It eventually occurred to me that every Wednesday morning we went to the supermarket at about ten a.m. We always entered via the back entrance, walking through the gardening department. There was a strong chemical odour in this section, presumably fertilisers. In the few minutes I spent passing through, or waiting at a till, I inhaled sufficient of these fumes to cause the chemical stress reaction. After that I kept out of the gardening section and had no more Wednesday headaches.

The discovery of chemical-pattern body stress has been a revelation. For most of my life I had experienced intense migraines, which came on for no reason. Lying down often intensified the pain, so I had been forced to use painkillers just to get through the following few days. Gradually the pain would fade, but my neck remained sensitive and made a grating sound when I turned my head. Now I have an awareness of many substances that cause the chemical stress reaction in me, and I avoid exposure to them. Sometimes chemical stress will sneak up on you. For example, I can be sitting in a restaurant when I feel the characteristic tightening occurring at the base of my skull, and I realise that some cleaning product or insecticide has been used in the environment. Not only do I leave as quickly as possible, but I do the specific releases on my neck right away. In this way the chemical reaction is stopped in its tracks, and does not progress to a pounding headache. On occasion, I have had Ewald do the releases on my neck in a shopping mall or other public place. The peculiar looks we get from passers-by are infinitely preferable to allowing the whole body stress pattern to lock in.

A girl of twelve experienced bouts of headaches and vomiting on a regular basis. After a lot of reflection her mother wondered whether it was significant that their house was next to a plant nursery. On speaking to the manager she discovered that her daughter became ill on the day of the week that the plants were sprayed with insecticide. With this information, she ensured that the child kept out of the garden on spraying days, and no longer inhaled the chemicals.

A woman in her forties was gradually overcome by an unknown illness – headaches, muscle weakness and exhaustion. Eventually she had to spend most of her time lying down. After several months, when medical conditions had been ruled out, the cause was discovered. Her illness had begun soon after new cupboards had been fitted in the bedroom. Some detective work led to the factory that supplied the boards. It turned out that the batch of board used had not been properly dried, so the anti-beetle agents were exuding constantly into the air. The woman immediately moved to another bedroom and the cupboards were dismantled. She recovered completely.

We had a client who had severe Friday evening headaches. It emerged that every Friday she attended a flower-arranging course, and she was reacting to the adhesive tape used in binding the stems together. She discovered that if she wore rubber gloves when using the tape there was no adverse effect.

Chemical stress may also result from the overuse of a substance, which in normal doses would cause no harm. At one time I started eating Brazil nuts every day, and after a few weeks I was having daily chemical headaches. I did not suspect the nuts as I had always eaten them with no ill effects. Eventually we worked out that they were causing the problem. After a year I was able to eat them again, but in moderation.

The BSR practitioner can assist in the detective work. While the client inhales or touches the suspect substance, the practitioner activates the biofeedback response, and observes whether the body reacts.

In one challenging case, we tested the toiletries and cleaning products used by a client. She stopped using the ones indicated by her body's responses, yet her headaches persisted. Each time we checked her for body stress, the typical chemical effect pattern was present. She finally came up with the answer herself. 'Could I be reacting to the anti-fungus spray my husband uses on his feet before going to bed?' This turned out to be true. When she instituted a banning order – against the spray, not the husband – it was the end of the headaches.

Viruses and infections

The chemical stress patterns are detectable when a person has a cold or flu – obviously from toxins formed within the body. After the releases, a high temperature usually plummets to normal. However, it climbs back up within the hour. We observed the battle between the body and the virus when we brought an elderly friend to stay at our house. She had a severe case of flu and felt she was getting worse every day, lying in the sickbay of the old-age home. We released the chemical stress pattern three times a day. Each time her temperature dropped dramatically, and then went up again as the virus regained the upper hand. By the third day her immune system won, and she was back to normal.

A similar process took place when Ewald had tick-bite fever. This disease usually causes an intense headache. Each time he felt the head pressure building up, I released the chemical stress pattern and the pain withdrew immediately.

Overheating

Some people are very sensitive to a hot climate and they react with heat exhaustion, which causes an intense headache. We see this as a form of chemical stress, as in every case of overheating we detect the typical chemical body stress patterns.

Multiple chemical sensitivities

People who are chemically sensitive are often regarded as neurotic. When they complain of the nausea and headaches caused by substances that do not seem to affect other people, they are seen as being overdramatic or inclined to exaggerate. Those who have not experienced chemical stress have no idea how much suffering it causes. The public needs to be made aware of the effects of being exposed to harmful chemicals, as the consequences may be life-altering. Cases have been documented in which people have been sensitised by a massive exposure to certain substances, such as a toxic spider bite or inhalation of solvents. This caused them to develop multiple chemical sensitivities, to the extent that they could no longer tolerate even low levels of everyday chemicals. They have been forced to withdraw from society and live in isolation, in order to survive.

CHAPTER 15

BSR's place in the health-care spectrum

BSR's relationship with medicine

Referrals from medicine

A paediatrician who had phoned for an appointment walked into our BSR practice cradling a five-month-old baby in his arms, followed by the baby's mother and grandmother. The little boy's arms were locked in a spasm against his chest, he kept moving his head, and his gaze was unfocused. The doctor said that no abnormalities had been seen on the neck X-ray, and he feared it may be a case of cerebral palsy. The parents of other patients had told him about our work. Before proceeding with brain scans, he wanted to see if BSR could help in any way.

The doctor watched while we released several areas of stress in the neck, as well as the lower back. When the mother brought the baby for his second appointment, the arms were normal and mobile, and to her joy he could now focus on her face and respond to her. We found a small area

of residual body stress in the neck. We did not see the baby or his mother again, as they returned to their home overseas. Six months later the grandmother sent a photograph of the little boy standing, and she described his development as normal in every way.

That was the start of many referrals from that paediatrician, and we felt appreciation for his confidence in BSR. Over the years a large number of medical doctors have recommended patients to BSR, not only GPs, but specialists such as orthopaedic surgeons, cardiologists, and dermatologists. There have been cases of patients who were scheduled for back surgery who responded so positively to BSR that the surgery was cancelled.

Leonard, aged fifty-two, had long-term, severe lower-back and left leg pain. After his first BSR session his coccyx was burning and the leg pain was worse. Over the next month he experienced good and bad days, while the pain decreased to some extent. However, he decided that he would prefer a quicker solution through spinal surgery, which his orthopaedic surgeon had suggested months before. The surgery was booked. At the pre-op check the day before, the surgeon informed Leonard that surgery was out of the question, and demanded to know what on earth he had been doing to be so improved. When told about BSR the surgeon advised him to 'keep it up'. Soon after that he was able to drive again. After eight more BSR sessions, eight months later, Leonard was fit and pain-free, and once again able to enjoy his favourite activities – hiking and cycling.

Some other types of surgery have been avoided after BSR. A sixty-year-old woman writes, 'I consulted with my gynaecologist and he reported that I presented with "classical stress incontinence for which a suprapubic bladder neck suspension operation is necessary". I had a history of lower-back problems and recalled that previously when I had Body Stress Release, the bladder problem had eased. I therefore consulted with my BSR practitioner. I had BSR attention for about six months. During this time I noted the improvement in my condition at various levels, and after five months my bladder control was normal. I consulted with my gynaecologist for a routine check-up, and after a physical examination he

was considerably impressed with the excellent progress achieved. He stated that an operation was certainly no longer required and that I should "continue doing whatever you have been doing". Thanks to the BSR practitioner for the "magic touch".

Besides the fact that they have heard about the effectiveness of BSR from their patients, we believe that medical practitioners have a sense of trust in BSR for several reasons. It is a gentle, non-invasive technique, so there is no fear of their patients being injured. It is complementary, not alternative to medicine. Those doctors who have experienced BSR themselves comment that its principles are very logical.

BSR enjoys a reciprocal relationship with other health practitioners, such as physiotherapists, fitness coaches, posture trainers, yoga teachers and psychologists, with referrals going both ways. Such practitioners frequently comment that clients who had reached a plateau in their progress make a leap forward after their body stress is released.

Complementary not alternative

These two terms are often used interchangeably, as in 'complementary medicine' or 'alternative health-care'. They are, in fact, two quite distinct approaches and should not be confused. 'Alternative' implies 'instead of', in other words, you attend an alternative practitioner in place of your medical doctor.

> BSR stands squarely under the title 'complementary'.

BSR stands squarely under the title 'complementary'. It is a health-care profession that works alongside medicine, in co-operation, not in competition. It can enhance function while the person is undergoing a medical treatment, e.g. a doctor sets a broken leg, and the BSR practitioner releases the body stress which locked into the back during the accident, or that results from walking in a cast.

The BSR practitioner does not in any way diagnose or treat conditions, nor give advice on the process of a disease – that is the field of medicine. BSR does not try to duplicate any part of medical services.

BSR is one of the founder members of COCHASA, the Confederation of Complementary Health Associations of South Africa, which was established in I992. This organisation represents those associations which uphold the principle of being non-therapeutic. The term 'therapy' is another word that is widely misused in the health-care realm. Its definition is 'concerned with the treatment and cure of diseases'. Thus a profession calling itself a therapy is placing itself in the arena of diagnosing and treating, which implies it is an alternative to medicine.

Scope of practice

BSR has a clear-cut scope of practice, and practitioners are bound by the BSR constitution to adhere to this. It is limited to the location and releasing of 'body stress', which is stored tension. It does not involve medication, machines or manipulation, therefore it does not invade any field of medical practice. Health-care professionals know that when they refer a patient to BSR, that person will not be subjected to anything outside of the scope of practice.

The BSR stance is that health practitioners of any kind should remain within their defined scope of practice, become expert in their limited field, and refer clients to other types of practitioners for any other procedures. Every profession has something of value to offer, or it would not exist. In choosing any health-care practitioner, one tends to have more confidence in practitioners who limit themselves to their technique, rather than in someone who offers a great range of procedures. A practitioner is unlikely to achieve excellence as a jack-of-all-trades.

BSR vocabulary

In order to avoid giving the false impression that any diagnosis or treatment of any condition is being offered, in BSR we avoid using terminology which may be misleading. We refer to a BSR session, consultation or appointment, and not a 'treatment'. The practitioner does a BSR assessment, not a 'diagnosis'. The words 'therapy' and 'therapist' are not used. We use the term 'client' and not 'patient'.

In this way BSR maintains its clear identity and its role as a complementary health-care profession.

Referrals to medicine

Most often clients have already undergone medical care before coming for BSR. However, in the process of assessing a client for body stress, if we notice something unusual, e.g. a strange lump, we tactfully point it out to the client, and ask if their medical doctor is aware of it. If the client says no, we suggest a medical check-up.

If, over a series of BSR sessions, clients mention new symptoms, or describe some condition as deteriorating, we urge them to consult their doctor. A young woman was experiencing pain in her lower back and abdomen. Over three appointments the lower-back ache eased but the abdominal pain worsened. The BSR practitioner advised her to see her doctor, who diagnosed an ectopic pregnancy and surgery was carried out.

Over the years in our practice we have seen a number of clients whose severe lower-back pain did not improve after several BSR sessions. We advised them to consult their doctor about a referral to a specialist, such as an orthopaedic surgeon. In a few of these cases, the specialists found that disc surgery was necessary. In others, the specialists referred the person back to us. They diagnosed the disc degeneration as not severe enough to warrant surgery, and recommended that the client continue with BSR for 'conservative management'.

Reduction of medication

Often medication such as painkillers or anti-inflammatories may be reduced or terminated after BSR. It is made clear to the client that medication should only be changed under the direction of the medical doctor or other health practitioner who prescribed it.

Twenty-five years of headaches

After twenty-five years of intense, constant, daily headaches, Bernard, aged sixty-six, relied on various medications in order to cope. He was taking anti-inflammatories, painkillers (up to twelve a day), anti-depressants and tranquillisers. He also complained of lower-back pain and occasional panic attacks. When the medication was no longer

effective, his GP referred him to a BSR practitioner. After the release of tension in his neck and lower back, his headaches and lower-back pain abruptly ceased. A mild headache occurred a week later.

On his fifth visit, his wife came with him to tell the practitioner about the 'massive emotional detoxification' Bernard had just gone through. A very severe headache had come on, and he had sat all day holding his head and sobbing like a child. For the first time he poured out the story of his traumatic childhood with an abusive mother.

Now Bernard has BSR for health maintenance, and only experiences an occasional twinge of head pain, which sometimes warrants a painkiller.

Arthritis of the spine

A thirty-year-old man tells his story: 'I was diagnosed with arthritis in my spine five months ago. My doctor informed me that it would require surgery. I was then referred to a BSR practitioner by my sister, who has been going for BSR for a year now. I was a bit sceptical and nervous. The practitioner immediately put me at ease by explaining the procedure. After four sessions I felt like a new person. I also had no more headaches or spastic colon. After my month of BSR I went back to my orthopaedic surgeon. He was amazed to find that I had fewer backaches. I no longer needed my medication.

My surgeon told me to become best friends with my Body Stress Release practitioner. I intend to go for my BSR once a month.'

High blood pressure

An ENT specialist, aged fifty-seven, decided to try BSR to deal with his lower-back and leg pain. As a medical doctor, at first he was very sceptical that such a non-invasive approach could have profound results. By his third session most of the pain had withdrawn, but he had

developed dizziness. As he was on medication for high blood pressure he said he would have a check-up with his physician. His blood pressure was found to have lowered so dramatically that his medication was reduced. By his sixth session he was free of the pain that had brought him to BSR, and as his blood pressure had normalised, his doctor terminated his medication. Naturally he continued to have his blood pressure checked on a regular basis.

Who is the healer?

BSR practitioners regard themselves as health practitioners, not healers. Only the wisdom of the body should be regarded as the healer. With this understanding, we see all forms of health-care as catalysts in the healing process, and remain in awe of the body's miraculous ability to heal and regenerate itself.

In BSR we do not claim to treat or cure anything. As BSR is aimed at enhancing the body's self-healing capacity, it works very well alongside medical treatment or other forms of health-care.

A medical doctor who was a guest speaker at a BSR conference expressed his admiration of the principles and effects of BSR. He concluded his lecture with this advice to practitioners, 'Stay amazed at the power in your hands – and don't get cocky!'

CHAPTER 16

How to avoid stress overload

There is a common saying, 'You don't cure stress, you manage it.' In Body Stress Release, we aim to help people to be more aware of the stress factors in their lives, and to make choices and changes in those areas which are within their control, thereby reducing the impact of the stress. Sometimes people may need 'quick fixes' to cope with a situation in the short term, but if they come to rely on these, they will be suppressing problems which will lead to functioning at a far lower level than they should.

Some of the advice that follows is common sense, while some may be surprising and possibly contrary to the actions and exercises you have been following.

Health has three facets: mechanical soundness, chemical well-being and mental and emotional balance. The degree to which we are able to avoid stress overload in all of these areas determines our level of health.

Mechanical stress

Except for accidents, we are entirely capable of controlling the amount and nature of the mechanical stress and strain to which our bodies are subjected daily. We need to be aware of our posture, whether sitting, standing, or carrying out various activities.

The lower back

The lower back is the foundation of the spine, and the key to avoiding stress overload is to 'preserve the curve'. The amount of pressure exerted on the discs of the spine varies according to our posture and body position. The moment we bend forward or hunch the back, whether sitting or standing, the load on the discs increases dramatically.

Sitting

When sitting, it is vital to avoid slumping, or sitting with the feet propped up. If the natural forward curve of the lumbar spine is flattened or reversed, pressure builds up on the front part of the discs between the vertebrae. Over time this may weaken the tough outer cartilage part, and the jelly-like centre of the disc may be forced backwards. This may result in a bulge developing in the disc wall, which could put pressure on a spinal nerve.

A person with lower-back pain often says, 'The only time I get any relief is when I half lie on the couch with my feet on the coffee table.' This is because that position reduces the pressure at the back of the disc, temporarily lessening any compression of the spinal nerve by the disc. However, the person is worsening the problem – the abnormal pressure placed on the front of the discs is aggravating the squeezing backwards of the disc material. When straightening up again the nerve compression and pain will recur.

The correct curve of the lower back is stabilised if the knees are level with or slightly lower than the hips. Avoid couches and chairs that are designed with a backward-sloping seat, causing the knees to be higher than the hips. As explained above, this rounding-out effect on the lumbar spine may feel comfortable for a short time, but will result in increased disc pressure. Most car seats are too low, but placing a cushion in the hollow of the back helps to maintain the curve.

Lifting

When lifting heavy objects, we should never bend forward. Instead we need to bend the knees, keep the spine straight and hold the object close to the body, allowing the thigh muscles to take the strain. Some lifting is a two-person job, e.g. a heavy table or television, with a person taking the weight on each side.

Sleeping

When it comes to sleeping, the quality of the mattress is important. Like Goldilocks' choice, it should not be too hard or too soft. A hard mattress does not support the lumbar curve. If a person finds a very hard mattress comfortable, it suggests that there is a great deal of body stress present in the lower back, causing the muscles to be locked into a spasm which has flattened out the natural curve. If a mattress is too soft, the spine will slump into a 'hammock' shape, leading to body stress. If the mattress does not have enough 'give' to mould to the spinal curves, it is helpful to place a thin cushion under the lower back.

Exercise

Obviously it is beneficial to pursue moderate and sensible forms of exercise, to strengthen muscles and make the body more resistant to mechanical stresses. Exercises which reverse the lumbar curve should be avoided, such as toe-touching, as well as twisting movements. Of course our spines are designed to be able to do these movements, without damage, when necessary. However, to perform them repeatedly and forcefully places extreme pressure on the inter-vertebral discs, which in time leads to degeneration. Other exercises that may strain the lower back are full sit-ups and lying on the back and raising both legs without bending them.

When body stress is present, vigorous exercise is not advisable.

Besides gym exercises which are performed with the correct lumbar curve, other good forms of exercise are walking, swimming, and cycling with good posture. Jumping on a rebounder (mini-trampoline) is very beneficial, so long as it is done moving from one foot to the other, not with both legs at once. If jogging is your favourite exercise, run on a sports field rather than subjecting your body

to the jarring effects of a rigid road surface and the inhalation of car exhaust fumes.

It is important to remember that when body stress is present, vigorous exercise is not advisable, as it merely reinforces the protective tightening of muscles. Once the stored tension has been released, and the muscles have relaxed back to normal tone, exercise will strengthen the muscles.

In doing sport and exercise, remember to listen to your body. Pain is a warning signal that you are starting to push yourself beyond your individual limit, into overload. Stop or adapt the activity – do not ignore the pain, or try to 'work through it', or suppress it with painkillers. Rest is important to avoid overload. Pay attention to your body's message that it is tired and needs sleep or relaxation. If you are a fitness enthusiast or sportsperson, naturally you aim to up your game, but develop an awareness of your capabilities so that you do not stretch yourself beyond your adaptability.

The neck

The structures of the neck are easily stressed. We should try to avoid having the head tilted down for long periods of time, as in reading with a book in the lap. Studying should be done at a table with the book propped up. Extreme twisting of the neck may lead to body stress – use the rear-view mirror when reversing a car. Do not sleep on your stomach, as this twists the neck. Sleep on your back with a fairly thin pillow which supports the curve of the neck, rather than a thick one which causes the chin to tilt down onto the chest. If you sleep on your side, fold the pillow double so that it fills in the space between your neck and the bed.

Some actions put the neck into stress overload almost immediately. A young woman came for BSR suffering from a very stiff, painful neck and headaches. I noticed she had very curly short hair, and asked if her hair had been permed before the problems started. She realised that they had begun a month before, immediately after the perming session. A perm involves sitting for a long time with the head tilted backwards, and the hard edge of the basin puts pressure on the neck. We recommend that a towel is used to pad the basin edge during the hairwashing process.

Working at a computer may induce body stress throughout the spine. Ensure that the chair is the correct height for you and that it supports your lumbar curve, and that the monitor is at a level which allows you to keep your neck upright.

Chemical stress

We are often subjected to chemical stress overload without being aware of it. Even if you are not chemically sensitive and do not experience the typical effects of chemical stress, such as headaches and neck pain, your body is still adversely affected by being exposed to harmful substances. Your liver, which is responsible for breaking down toxins, may be put under strain, as well as your kidneys, which have the task of clearing undesirable chemicals from your system.

As described before, there are three ways in which a harmful substance enters the body – we may eat or drink it, breathe it in, or absorb it through the skin.

Consumption

It makes sense to follow a balanced and varied diet and exclude any foods to which you have an adverse reaction. Try to eat foods in a form as close as possible to their original state. Read the contents labels on processed foods, and if possible avoid those containing artificial colourants and flavour-enhancing substances. Check the fine print – the words 'natural' or 'organic' may refer to only a small percentage of the contents.

To avoid consuming insecticides, always peel fruit unless you are sure that it is organically grown. Do not buy fruit and vegetables that look oversized, as growth-stimulating chemicals may have been used. Be alert to how you feel after eating something new. If your neck muscles start tightening and you develop a headache, suspect that the food contained some additive to which you are sensitive. It may be a product that looks quite innocuous, such as a creamy filling in a biscuit or pie. You may find that you react to certain brands of food or drink, such as wines, and not to others.

Inhalation

Have you ever sat next to someone wearing a strong perfume or aftershave lotion, and developed a throbbing headache? Try to avoid breathing in fumes of any kind. If you are forced to use harsh chemicals, such as insecticide sprays or cleaning fluids, hold your breath and remove yourself from the environment immediately. Many people cannot tolerate being in a room where a chemical was sprayed even hours before. When using paints or varnishes, keep doors and windows open to minimise the fumes.

Contact

If using the sprays mentioned above, make sure that they do not come into contact with your skin. You may be subjected to chemical stress through touch when you least expect it – I once developed a chemical-type headache after arranging a bunch of flowers. Some form of chemical must have been sprayed onto the flowers. In choosing products used on the skin – cosmetics, toiletries, deodorants, etc. – each time you buy a new product, be aware of any neck tension or head pressure building up. Before investing in an expensive product, if possible take a sample home to try.

Mental and emotional stress

A teacher, Harry, was supervising a class of fourteen- and fifteen-year-old boys. One boy, labouring over his homework, asked, 'Sir, is geography important?' This opened the door for Harry to pose the question to the class, 'What is the most important thing in life?' The boys bombarded him with suggestions – career, money, success, friendship, family. Harry acknowledged the value of all these things, although they were not of ultimate importance. 'Please, sir, tell us what it is,' the teenagers begged as the school bell rang. 'The most important thing in life,' said Harry, 'is to have peace of mind, and how you achieve it is up to you.' The boys looked puzzled, too young to grasp the profundity of this insight.

If we can attain peace of mind, the mental and emotional stresses of life will cease to overwhelm us. The path to this state of emotional balance and inner peace is unique to each person. We all need to seek out and pursue whatever activities and techniques help us, individually, to reach this. For some it may be creative expression, such as art or writing, for others it is meditation, prayer, visualisation exercises, relaxation techniques or talking issues through with a friend or counsellor.

Physical approaches may help to deal with emotional stress, like playing sport, dancing or having a massage. Spending time in nature or listening to music can lessen the impact of mental and emotional stress.

Our belief system

At the various life stages it is helpful to take time to re-examine your life. Are you bored, frustrated, or unfulfilled? What are your values, your priorities, your goals? Have they changed, and do you need to make new choices in order to enrich your life?

You may become aware that your path in life has been determined by how you have been programmed by your parents, your education, peers and society.

At the age of thirty-eight, Marion had a revelation. 'I have just realised that as far back as I can remember I have been conducting my life according to my father's principles. In fact, we are very different people – I don't have the same values as him. What an unnecessary strain – trying to live up to ideas I don't believe in. No more!'

How we experience life is a direct result of what we believe. It is a circular process: our beliefs give rise to our attitudes, which create our feelings, which dictate what choices we make, and these determine the experiences we have, and in turn our experiences reinforce our beliefs.

For example, if you assume that a certain person does not like you, you will feel threatened or angry, so you are likely to act towards him in a defensive or belligerent way, and no doubt he will respond by being rude to you, thereby confirming your conviction that he is against you. So you have just created an ongoing stressful relationship.

There is a powerful saying, 'Where attention goes, energy flows; where energy flows, capacity grows.' If we focus on negative events and situations, they will increase and come to dominate our life. It is possible to train ourselves to observe our thoughts and stop our destructive self-talk in its tracks. Our minds, just like our bodies, need constant conditioning to stay in shape.

So much that we experience seems beyond our control. We may not be able to change a negative situation, but we can aim at altering our perception of it, and therefore our response. We need to become aware of our automatic responses to stressful situations, and relax hunched shoulders and tightened abdominal and jaw muscles, and take deep, slow breaths.

In the three arenas of health − mechanical, chemical, and mental or emotional − it is necessary to become conscious of the causes of stress overload that are affecting us as individuals. This enables us to make choices that empower us to upgrade the quality of our life expression.

In all aspects of our life, we should not ignore the warning signals that our bodies give us, alerting us that we are heading towards stress overload. A (hopefully) fictional story illustrates this:

A jumbo jet was about to take off when the pilot became aware of a knocking sound coming from one engine. He was very concerned, so he shut down the engines and informed the airline authorities. Take-off was delayed for several hours, as it took a long time to find another pilot.

CHAPTER 17

Clients' personal stories

What motivates BSR practitioners? They chose this career because their focus in life is helping others, and their greatest satisfaction is seeing the positive impact they are having on their clients' health and life in general. The most powerful affirmation for a practitioner is having clients express the wish to put their personal story in writing, so that it can inspire and reassure others who are experiencing similar problems.

This chapter contains accounts of people's experiences with BSR, in their own words. Names have been changed to preserve their privacy.

Epilepsy in a child

This was written by the parents of Eric, aged thirteen:

Eric was diagnosed with epilepsy at the age of five. He had no seizures, but an EEG revealed abnormal electrical activities in the brain. At the age of eight he had his first grand-mal seizure. A slow release anti-epileptic drug was prescribed, which kept the seizures under control.

At the age of twelve the seizures were no longer under control. He had a series of nine or ten at a time, every three weeks, and had to be hospitalised due to the fact that he went 'into status' and lost consciousness. This was life-threatening.

Over a five-month period he had about sixty seizures. He was then admitted to the epilepsy unit at a clinic in Cape Town for twenty-four-hour video monitoring. The neurologist–epileptologist discovered that his epilepsy originated from both lobes in the brain and during a seizure scatters all over the brain. An operation was done in which an incision was made between the two lobes. This would lessen the severity and had a 50 per cent chance to stop the seizures completely.

After seven weeks in Cape Town he returned to our home town. Five weeks after the operation, he had his first mild seizure.

The following year we heard about Body Stress Release and contacted a practitioner. She explained to us how the body relates to stress and anxiety. Her words were, 'I cannot cure the epilepsy but BSR may help his body to control it.' After seeing her he had two mild seizures. He has had releases every two weeks. During the December holidays, he had a four-week time span without releases and is still going strong. The BSR has definitely helped to give him a better quality of life. He has had a year free of hospitalisation and could go back to school.

The intensity of the seizures is far less. He is more relaxed and alert and his sleeping pattern has changed dramatically from very restless (turning, tossing, mumbling) throughout the night, to the minimum movement and the odd sleep-talking.

We are definitely sticking to frequent BSR sessions to try to keep the epilepsy under control. The doctors have said Eric can be weaned off the medication when he is a year epilepsy-free. Bravo to Body Stress Release!

Practitioner's comment: Six months later Eric still has not had a seizure.

Body numbness
Mrs M., aged thirty-six, writes:

I've been suffering for more than six years with a numbness on the left side of my body. It affected my neck right down to my foot. I've been to a number of doctors, and their diagnoses were: muscle spasm, inflamed muscles and even arthritis. I went for heart tests as well as a mammogram, but to no avail. Someone referred me to Body Stress Release and I thought that I'd try it to see how and if it worked. I was amazed and absolutely overjoyed at the results. The numbness went away gradually and the technique really worked for me.

Presently I feel much better, and to think that I've actually spent quite a large amount of money for six years. I went through agony and felt very depressed. I am so excited at this moment because I can truly say that BSR works. I feel how the body heals itself. I would also recommend people with any physical problem to have Body Stress Release.

A dramatic change in vision

Ebrahim, aged sixty-seven, wrote after his first BSR session:

A miracle has happened in my life! I got home after my first BSR visit, sat down, exhausted, as you said I would be, turned on the TV and felt around for my specs. I couldn't find them, but thought it wouldn't really matter, because I knew I was going to fall asleep within minutes. Then I looked up at the TV … and, for the first time in my life, I could see the screen perfectly without my specs, which I have had to wear for nearly sixty-six years.

Practitioner's comment: When Ebrahim came for BSR he complained of lower-back, neck and abdominal pain, as well as pain and tingling in his fingers, and constipation. He had experienced headaches 'for years'. He had undergone three eye operations between the ages of eight and twelve, and was wearing thick lens spectacles.

By his fourth visit he reported that he had almost no headaches any more, his tummy was working well, his hands and fingers were fine – in fact he was almost 100 per cent. I encouraged him to return to his specialist for an eye check. 'You have 20/20 vision!' said the amazed specialist. 'I'm not even going to give you reading specs.'

The baby who cried constantly

Sean's mother reports:

Sean was born on a Monday. On the Thursday we attempted to leave the hospital for hours, but failed to do so as Sean cried continuously. The paediatrician at the hospital said that he most likely had cramps or he was very warm due to the high temperature of the air conditioner in the room. Being first-time parents we felt helpless and confused.

Sean continued to cry for a couple of hours when we got home and we eventually managed to get him to sleep. On Friday he cried for

most of the day and I decided to phone my BSR practitioner to arrange a session as I assumed that Sean probably had stress in his body due to the birth. The practitioner was fully booked for the day but kindly accommodated us at 6.30 that evening. My husband and myself took Sean to the practitioner, who worked on him by placing him on my chest. A lot of stress was found, especially on the area linked to his stomach, and releases were done on his spine.

There was a major change in Sean after that. He settled down very nicely and he slept more soundly and for longer periods. We had a follow-up visit five days later and the practitioner found there was a big improvement with little or no stress on most areas on the spine.

I would highly recommend Body Stress Release to young and old as it definitely works. I have been having BSR sessions for the past seven years. I used to suffer from lower-back pain. I very seldom have it now, and if I do get any stress in my back, just one session will fix me up for a couple of months. I have also been relieved of back pain resulting from breastfeeding and bad posture while holding the baby.

Sean has just turned three months old and I will continue to take him for BSR in the future.

Intense neck pain
This is Pieter's experience:

In December I was given a fright and my whole body jerked. The result of the jerk was a pain that shot through my shoulder to my neck. From that moment on I had a constant and unbearable pain that did not ease off.

I consulted my doctor the next day, and he immediately had X-rays taken and referred me to a specialist. The specialist recommended that I should have a CAT scan, but this was out of the question as my medical aid was exhausted and there was no way that I could afford the cost. He arranged for me to hire a traction unit to relieve the pain.

However, this was a short-term arrangement and did not really work. I was thinking of various options for assistance, including surgery, which scared me. I went away on a caravan holiday and spent the entire time in the caravan tent in traction, pain and suffering.

Back home I was told about BSR and with mixed feelings I phoned and made an appointment. During the session I could hardly lie on the bed owing to the severe pain. The next day I recall telling my wife that the pain was not as severe. With my second visit three days later, I could lie still and tell the practitioner as she worked with me where it was sensitive. I had been unable to do this during the first session. I again returned after three weeks and had remarkable results – no pain, and I mean without any pain. Now after five sessions I do not know what shoulder pain is, how wonderful! I definitely will go back on a monthly basis for maintenance. I also will recommend BSR to anybody.

My thanks to my practitioner – words cannot express my appreciation. I wish you well with Body Stress Release, I wish upon you God's richest blessing and pray that many more people like myself will find relief and benefit from your help and dedication.

A motorbike accident
Michelle's story:

I would like to tell my story about the miracle that was performed with a little help from my Body Stress Release practitioner and his miracle hands.

I made the mistake of getting on the back of a motorbike of a friend who was emotionally unstable, and consequently was involved in an accident. He got away with a few scratches, but I was not as fortunate. I ended up in hospital. Three days later I was released as nothing was broken, and the doctors could not do much more for me apart from pumping me full of painkillers. I had injured my back in a previous accident, and it hurt again. I also had to wear a neck brace.

I was in constant pain in my lower back, my left leg and my neck. But the worst was the fact that I could only move my right arm about two centimetres away from my body. There was no way that I could even try lifting it. I was, to say the least, completely devastated, and being a waitron, I needed the use of my arm as well as being able to be quick on my feet, and here I was, hardly able to move.

The doctors told me that I wouldn't be able to work for at least two months, that I had to wear a neck brace for about the same period of time, and that I would need at least six months of physiotherapy. Apart from not being able to work, I could not play darts (my big passion) any more. I started suffering severe headaches, sleepless nights and complete lack of appetite. Only later was I to realise the cause.

I saw a friend about nine days after the accident. He was horrified to see the state I was in, especially as I had cut my long hair. I explained that I was suffering doing simple day-to-day chores, even as simple as washing my hair – with one hand. He asked how open-minded I was and told me about Body Stress Release. I was so desperate that I was willing to try anything.

I was very sceptical, but as I said before, I was frustrated, irritated and in pain. I was going to give anything a go as long as I got better. The BSR practitioner explained what he does and how it all works. To this day, the one thing he said that still stands out is the fact that, and here I'm going to quote: 'Your brain has a blueprint of your body from when it was born. I'm just helping it to remember.'

After he lowered me on his bed and got to work, he talked to me all the while, to put me at ease. He explained that everything in your body is connected. During the accident I must have experienced trauma, not just to my body, but psychologically and emotionally as well. All the symptoms I was experiencing were linked.

I walked out of his rooms still in pain, but feeling a lot better. Over the next few weeks I saw the practitioner often, and he became my

salvation. After only four weeks I was back at work and was also able to play darts again. I found that, apart from recovering full use of my body, I was also able to concentrate better.

During this period I came to learn a lot about how one's body works and I came to understand how it responds to stress. Small things stress us out and we don't even realise it. I learned that stress can turn to depression, and that turns to more stress. A vicious circle that can only be broken if you release the stress in your life and avoid the causes. I've come to realise how precious our bodies are and how easily we take them for granted – that is, until we break them down, of course. Since I've been having Body Stress Release I've noticed a few changes in myself. I am a lot more confident, secure and at peace with myself.

I will continue having BSR, and I will recommend it to anybody. Take it from me, the big sceptic. I want to say thank you to my practitioner, not only for your miracle hands, but for your positive outlook and cheerful smile.

Rheumatoid arthritis
David sent a handwritten account of his recovery back to fitness:

As a senior citizen I am happy to lead an active life and to know that I still make a meaningful contribution to society.

This was not the case some two years ago when various physical problems started to limit my mobility. Carpal tunnel release surgery was indicated to be necessary (both hands). This relieved some discomfort but my hands would not obey and the level of pain restricted usage. Eventually rheumatoid arthritis was diagnosed and new medication was indicated. This was not the way I planned to spend my retirement – there was so much I wanted to do.

At this point I was encouraged to try Body Stress Release to assist the body to help itself. This I did. Now after one-and-three-quarter years of monthly sessions it's difficult to think back to what it was like with all that discomfort. During this time symptoms of rheumatoid

arthritis have disappeared, my feet grew one size larger and I can again lift my right arm. My hands are willing to execute functions and writing is no longer an impossibility. Swollen large joints are back to normal and the left and right brain are functioning in synchrony!

A recent visit to an ophthalmologist showed that glaucoma (diagnosed two years earlier) had disappeared, confirmed in three successive visits over four weeks. Medication has been terminated. I knew that certain prescribed medicines had brought on the initial problems, but it was not so easy to convince the medical caretakers that a change of prescription was called for. I was fortunate in finding a physician who was prepared to listen and implement changes. I was even more fortunate to meet up with a BSR practitioner who assisted my body to release the muscles from their defensive stress.

Continued selected exercises throughout this difficult time with a biokineticist was a great help and support. During early morning gym sessions we now have great fun looking back to a time when every movement was a problem.

May my return to fitness be an encouragement to those who have a problem with their body, to seek out the help that will assist them to overcome it. Also, a word of thanks to those who wish to help and know they can make a difference.

Migraines and painkillers
Patrick describes his search for relief:

After twenty years of suffering with headaches that ordinary analgesics would not touch, I went to a neurologist who diagnosed classical migraines and prescribed one of the new drugs. This drug was effective and removed the headache within two hours, but was very expensive and not covered by my medical aid, and the headaches continued. After two further years of continued headaches, during which time the migraine drug became less effective, I went back to the neurologist.

He diagnosed rebound headaches in which the various pills were aggravating the headaches rather than improving them. The only solution to this was to stop taking all analgesics for three months after which my system would have returned to normal.

This sounded like a drastic step and one that I probably would be unable to cope with as my job required prolonged periods of concentration and work at a computer. With the Christmas break and a period of leave approaching I decided to try a less drastic solution: to stop using the migraine drug, to try not to take analgesics and to take one and not two if essential, to find more time for exercise, and to take a break rather than a pill when a headache developed. Also, at my wife's prodding, I went to a Body Stress Release practitioner. It is now three months later and I have not taken any more of the migraine drugs, and while I still get headaches from time to time, they are not as intense as they were. Which, if any, of the lifestyle changes is responsible for the reduction in headaches is unclear to me, but I view BSR as an important part of treatment and will continue to go once a month.

A BSR practitioner's perspective

My first experience of BSR was in 1983 and having had neck problems my whole life (I was a forceps delivery) I can honestly say that it has been BSR that has allowed me the quality of life I've been able to enjoy and maintain. I've learned so much about trusting the body's natural healing mechanism, and understanding so much more about biomechanics and what can be potentially harmful, and what can be done to maintain as best as possible a healthy state. The guidance we can offer as practitioners is as important as the releasing we do.

I've had my own fair share of sports injuries – shoulder dislocations, torn hamstrings, teeth knocked out, two neck compressions, crushed knuckle, broken metacarpals and ribs. Some of these resulted in excruciating arm pain from nerve irritations and at times spasmed upper-back muscles causing indescribable discomfort. BSR relieved the pain and enhanced my body's recovery from these injuries.

I've had golfers that have come to me thinking that they will never play again – they've played and are still playing; I've had 'frozen' shoulders 'unfreeze'; I've had colicky babies sleeping through the night; I've had headache sufferers forgetting what that was like; I've had limping elderly ladies walking with a lot less pain and stiffness.

I could go on and on. BSR is the most wonderful technique. It facilitates the body's healing mechanism and creates an environment in which the body can more readily reach its homeostatic balance.

I am in the sixtieth year and have a level of fitness and health that would not have been as easily achievable without BSR.

Practical miracles: cases from practitioners' records

People choose to undergo Body Stress Release for a variety of reasons. The most common motivation is to find relief from symptoms like pain and stiffness. However, as nearly all clients go to a practitioner as a result of a personal referral from a friend, relative or a health practitioner, they often have an understanding from these people's experiences that BSR has a more profound purpose: as communication is restored within the body, it is enabled to function more efficiently. Therefore people who seek out BSR are hoping for an upgrading of their body's ability to deal with a wide range of health issues and conditions.

In every case the BSR practitioner carries out the body stress tests in order to locate the sites of stored tension, and release the body stress. The clients' symptoms are not 'treated' in any way. It is a constant source of pleasure to the practitioner to hear from the clients how their bodies respond, and to see so many 'natural miracles' occurring.

In everyday practice, practitioners observe the minor miracles of pain withdrawing and mobility being restored. The cases described in this chapter relate to more dramatic and life-changing effects which clients have experienced.

However, not everyone experiences such profound results from BSR. It is important to be aware that a complex of factors is involved in the presence of body stress and the releasing process is different for everyone. For some, the responses are rapid while for others progress may be slow.

The extent to which the self-healing is carried out varies in individuals. Clients report a range of effects – for some there is complete or partial recovery of their health, while others may experience lesser or minimal changes.

Scoliosis: the girl with the 'S' bend in her back

Scoliosis is a sideways curvature of the spine. It may be congenital due to some deformity of the vertebrae, or the result of a disease or muscular imbalance.

BSR does not attempt to straighten abnormal curves in the spine. The whole spine is tested for stored tension, whether above or below the deviation, or within it. It is then up to the body to use the improved nerve communication and muscle tone to restore normal posture.

Claire is eight years old and was diagnosed with scoliosis when she was two-and-a-half. Although she did not complain of pain and was very active, doing gym at school, and swimming and judo, her parents were concerned that her distorted posture would worsen over time. The grandmother suggested that they try BSR.

Her BSR practitioner describes Claire as small for her age. She had a curvature to the right in her neck and to the left in her lower back. Both

shoulders appeared raised, and there was a slight hunchback between her shoulder blades. The first two sessions were fairly easy for the little girl – the hunched area was flatter, and she said that she had some pain in her arms when writing, a slight ache in her whole back, a 'burny feeling' in her upper legs and an 'empty feeling' in her belly. She agreed to stop the judo and gym for the time being.

However, over the next five BSR sessions Claire showed how brave she was, as the level of pain escalated with sensation being restored to numbed nerves. At times she was so exhausted that her eyes looked sunken and she could not go to school. But her spine responded dynamically and her parents saw the curvature in her neck disappear, while the one in the lower back bent slightly in the opposite direction before straightening. During this period she grew one centimetre in height. Her mother admitted she had been sceptical watching the release procedures, and had thought, 'Is that all? A little prod or jab here and there?'

After nine sessions Claire declared that she liked the releases and gave her practitioner a drawing of a clenched fist with the thumb pointing upwards, with, 'It goes very well with my back!' written underneath. On Claire's advice, her mother is starting to undergo BSR, as she also has scoliosis.

In some cases the straightening of the spine has been observed on X-ray. At fifteen, Tracey was diagnosed with scoliosis, and gave up dancing because of her back pain. After several sessions of BSR the pain had subsided, she was more flexible and went back to her dance classes. After six months she had a second X-ray, and the surgeon found that the curvature had reduced by between twelve and fourteen degrees.

In another case of scoliosis, a nine-year-old girl had BSR over a period of ten weeks. The 'S' bend reduced, her neck pain ceased, the ridge of muscle which had developed on one side in her lower back flattened, and the right shoulder blade became level with the left one. The child is now much happier and no longer feels self-conscious in summer clothes.

Diabetes: revival in the sixties

A BSR practitioner recounts the story of Maarten and Graham, who were in their mid-sixties.

Maarten was overweight, had diabetes mellitus, succumbed to pneumonia at least twice a year, and was decidedly grumpy. He came for BSR because his feet had been numb for forty-five years and he also suffered from chronic indigestion – even drinking a glass of water caused intense discomfort.

Graham had a painful lower back. He was obese, smoked at least sixty cigarettes a day and also had diabetes.

These gentlemen lived together and shared the most astounding diet. Besides all their other fatty favourites, they each heartily enjoyed a packet of bacon every morning for breakfast. Neither of them took any form of exercise; Maarten because his feet were too uncomfortable and Graham because he was simply too overweight. Generally they were both very unhealthy individuals.

After one BSR session Maarten's indigestion had improved so much he could hardly believe it. After six weeks of BSR the feeling in his feet had returned completely – no more pins and needles or numbness. One can fully appreciate his astonishment, as he had undergone every medical test and intervention available. In Holland during the war the doctors had even broken his toes in an attempt to resolve the problem. Now, by releasing the compression of body stress in his lower back, there was a more efficient flow of nerve and blood supply to his feet.

Graham's lower-back pain improved considerably. Understandably, they were both thrilled with the results of BSR. They decided that they would come for BSR maintenance, having releases every two weeks. Besides their improved health, it was wonderful to observe how much more positive they became about life in general.

One day, about two years after their first BSR appointments, they came into the practice room laughing like two little excited boys. They told their story: at their annual health check with their physician, she tested their urine samples with the 'sugar sticks', declared them to be faulty, and took out a new box of sticks. These were evidently not

working either, so she took blood samples and sent them off to the pathology lab for testing.

The results of these tests astonished everyone. Maarten and Graham no longer had diabetes. Their doctor was confused, but they were delighted. They said they knew BSR had assisted their bodies to heal themselves of their chronic conditions.

Their cases illustrate some basic principles of BSR: tension stored in the lower back may adversely affect the healthy functioning of the legs and feet. Such tension may remain locked into the body for decades. By releasing this body stress, the body is assisted to heal itself in more ways than one would have imagined – in both cases the capacity of the pancreas to produce adequate insulin had been revived.

The evidence in these cases would not have been quite as conclusive if:
▶ only one of them had had diabetes,
▶ they had not lived together and eaten the same diet,
▶ they had not both come regularly for BSR maintenance.

Their faith in BSR was sealed and they continued with their sessions. Ten years later, they appeared at least ten years younger than when I had first met them. They enjoyed regular exercise and had even improved their eating habits to a degree.

Burning and numbness: the half kiss that became whole

If you are seventy years old, your feet are burning and your toes are numb, you have painful leg cramps and pins and needles in your hands, it would be understandable if you were depressed and bad-tempered. But this is not the case with Dan – his BSR practitioner describes him as a man with an amazing love for life and a great sense of humour.

He is a retired road construction worker and paramedic, and spends his time fixing cars and motorbikes, and milking the cows on his smallholding.

In his first BSR session, tension was located throughout his spine, including over his coccyx. Each time the practitioner found a stressed site, Dan remarked, 'That's the spot my girlie,' or, 'You go for it,' and, 'I can't believe those little hands of yours are so strong.' Some of his comments were so amusing she had to concentrate hard to resist bursting out laughing.

At his second visit he walked in with a huge grin and told the story of the half kiss. Forty years ago, a sliver of metal shot up from a grinder and hit him in the lower lip, and he lost all feeling in one side of the lip. He joked that all these years he has only been able to give his wife a half a kiss. On the morning after the release session, he woke up with a tingling feeling in his lower lip, and when he leaned over to kiss his wife, he had 100 per cent feeling. 'Since then I haven't stopped kissing her.'

He no longer had burning under his feet, and his toes had life in them again. His body felt 'loose' with only some sensitivity in his lower back.

At his third appointment he was literally jumping up and down, saying he had no more cramping in his legs, and he could go down on his haunches again to crouch under the cars. Dan decided he would like to come for health maintenance once a month, as he said BSR had performed a miracle in his life.

Eczema

In this skin condition there is an itchy red rash, with small blisters that ooze and become crusted.

An office worker in her fifties, Laura said she had to change her bed sheets every morning as she always woke to find them covered in blood. Besides the eczema, she had diarrhoea, headaches, intermittent pins and needles in one arm, and pain and stiffness in her back and legs. She had been diagnosed with systemic lupus erythematosus, an autoimmune disease. She was on tranquillisers and antidepressants, and receiving counselling from a psychologist.

After her first BSR session her headaches were worse, although her neck was more flexible and the eczema less itchy. By her third visit she said that she had to change the sheets only once in three days. Over the next few sessions the headaches and diarrhoea were sometimes worse, and at times improved. The eczema cleared, then returned, and by the twenty-seventh day it disappeared entirely.

Laura said it was hard to believe that 'something which felt like a fairy dancing over my back' could have such an impact.

Spinal rods: less is more

Paul was in a serious car accident in 1994. He had such extensive spinal fractures that it was necessary to fuse the vertebrae surgically. In addition, rods were screwed into the bones on each side of the spine, all the way from the second cervical vertebra at the top of the neck, down to the second lowest vertebra (the fourth lumbar).

Ten years later this executive in his late fifties began experiencing back and neck pain. The medical investigation found that the rods had cracked, and there was osteoarthritis in his neck, as well as a prolapse of the disc below the fifth lumbar vertebra. He was told that surgery was out of the question, as too much damage would be caused in removing the rods. Anti-inflammatory medication was prescribed, as well as various physical therapies.

Seven months passed and Paul was now in extreme pain, unable to walk, sit or sleep. The pain over his lower back radiated into both legs and feet. His neck was rigid, his hands felt numb, and the headaches were severe. At this stage he finally consented to follow his wife's advice to see her BSR practitioner.

As BSR does not work on parts of the body that have implants, the only areas that could be tested for body stress and released were the top of the neck, the cranial bones, the fifth lumbar vertebra and sacroiliac joints. In spite of this limitation, the effects were astounding. Paul started feeling improvement after the first session, and by the

fourth most of the pain had withdrawn. At times he felt a re-tightening over his lower back, causing discomfort, so he had a BSR session every three weeks. He began doing the gentle muscle-strengthening exercise recommended by the practitioner, and now has a BSR maintenance check every three to four months.

Paul's quality of life has transformed, and he is once again able to go on regular hikes. So the question remains: how could such limited releases have such a profound effect, especially on such a difficult and unusual condition? The answer must be: the body has its wisdom, and knows how to take a minimal input and maximise the benefit.

Exhaustion: nine years of premature old age

As a military policeman, Bob was expected to maintain a high level of fitness and participate in various sports with his colleagues. At forty-seven he was struggling to keep up this macho façade, and hide the fact that he was in constant pain. Exhausted at the end of each day, he went to bed at 9 p.m. All he could do on the weekends was rest, to gather some strength to face Monday again. His marriage was under pressure as he had no energy left for his wife.

His sudden descent into this state of 'old age' had happened eight years before. A truck crashed into the back of his car, leaving him with severe back and neck pain. He was put on a rehabilitation programme. While exercising on a rowing machine, he felt something crack in his back, and he collapsed, unconscious. X-rays showed nothing, but an MRI scan taken six weeks later revealed a disc herniation at L5-S1 level (the base of the spine). Physical treatment seemed to settle this problem, but the neck pain continued. Many different approaches were tried over the next three years, but as there was no change he was told he would have to live with the pain.

By chance Bob's wife met a BSR practitioner, and her discussion with him led her to persuade her husband to make three appointments. Bob's entire spine had ridges of tight muscles with intense sensitivity

between his shoulder blades. By the second session he felt worse – a constant headache, no energy at all, and his old lower-back pain had returned. The practitioner assured him these were all positive signs that his body was releasing the years of compression, and his energy was being channelled into the healing process. By the third appointment, the lower-back pain had cleared but the neck pain still persisted.

The BSR tests showed that deeper pressure from the old whiplash accident was surfacing, and could be dealt with. That was the breakthrough. A few days later Bob's neck was fully mobile and pain-free, and he had no more headaches. He felt an overwhelming surge of energy, and an urge to recoup the nine years he had lost. His reclaimed youth manifested in two ways – his wife was radiantly happy and he bought a new car – a sports model.

Chemotherapy

In her early sixties, Elaine, a writer, was diagnosed with bone cancer. She was in agony and could not walk without the aid of crutches. She often used a wheelchair when exhaustion overcame her. In a six-week period she had six seizures, which left her unconscious for two days. She was now undergoing chemotherapy, and was depressed and very emotional.

Besides general muscular ache, when she consulted a BSR practitioner she had pain in one arm and in one leg. As she was so sensitive, very slight pressure was used in the releases. Although she felt light-headed and extremely tired afterwards, within two days her arm and leg pain were reduced, and her sleeping was improved. She arrived for her second session using only one crutch, as she still limped slightly. She was smiling and her complexion had a pink glow.

Two visits later she had discarded the crutch and walked briskly into the practice saying 'Well come on girl, let's get to it.' She reported that she was sleeping through the night and had started driving again. The

practitioner found that Elaine could now tolerate firmer pressure during the release process.

Perhaps the most uplifting effect was the change in her emotional state. Her depression had lifted and she was inspired to write again. In eight months she has written three children's books and returned to lecturing. Her oncologist is amazed that her condition has stabilised so dramatically.

In the case of serious disease, BSR has a supportive role to play and may provide relief from pain and discomfort. The wife of a man dying of cancer said that BSR was the one thing that brought him some comfort and ease in his last few weeks.

A 'very hard case' of infertility

So many health problems may be traced back to a childhood accident. The resulting body stress remains stored for years or even decades, disturbing the nervous system and causing an array of symptoms which come to be accepted as just the way things are.

Karien had lived with pain in her hips her whole life, ever since the age of five, when she fell off a tractor and it ran over her back. Now, at thirty-one, she suffered from a wide range of problems, in spite of being a very active farmer's wife. Her main complaints were pain in the neck and shoulder blades, and headaches. In addition, she had numb fingers at times, pain in the lower back, frequent calf and hamstring cramps, cold feet, and indigestion.

By her fourth BSR session only sensitivity in her spine remained. She confided to her practitioner that she had been desperately trying to conceive, without success, and her periods were very irregular. She was advised to have a BSR 'maintenance' session once a month, as well as whenever she found she was ovulating.

It happened that Karien's fourth such session coincided with her ovulation. She said she had been to a fertility clinic and had been

pronounced 'a very hard case'. The specialists had ordered a number of blood tests, and were awaiting the results in order to decide what course of action to take.

A month later at the fertility clinic her blood and hormonal tests were repeated, and a pregnancy test came up negative. The doctor again expressed grave doubts about the possibility of her ever conceiving, but he suggested hormonal treatment. Karien was very depressed, and did not take the prescription. Then her despondency transformed into delight a week later when she discovered that she was pregnant. The pregnancy test had given a false negative.

At her next BSR check, she backtracked her date of conception to the day of or the day after her last BSR session. She continued to have regular BSR during the pregnancy and gave birth to a boy.

This BSR practitioner reports that she has had four other cases of women battling infertility, all of whom conceived 'coincidentally' on the day of or the day after their BSR session. She comments, 'Body Stress Release will never, ever cease to amaze me.'

Brain damage and paralysis

In one shattering moment, just as she was stepping into the freedom of adulthood, Theresa was slammed shut in the prison of her body. A car accident, causing extensive brain damage, left this nineteen-year-old girl paralysed. She could not speak, she had no control over her arms and legs, and her parents had to carry her. Propped up in a chair, her body was twisted to one side and she would slide into a slump. Her neck muscles were contracted, pulling her chin onto her chest. Her right foot was twisted onto its outer edge, and spasm of the leg muscles kept her left foot hooked behind the other ankle. Having lost all control of her bladder she had to wear nappies, and with no bowel movement, it was necessary for her mother to clean out her colon manually every few days.

She was taken for therapy and her mother performed passive exercise of her limbs, but her condition remained unchanged for the

next three years, except for one advance – she started uttering a few words, with great effort, which only her mother could understand.

Her parents were told about BSR, and over the next four years Theresa had a release session about once a month, with occasional longer intervals between appointments. There have been many changes, showing that, with spinal nerve compression being reduced, many sensory and motor pathways are being re-activated:

▶ The neck muscles relaxed and she can raise her head.
▶ The lumbar spine, which was rounded into a humped shape, has restored its forward curve.
▶ Sensation has returned to her legs, with feelings of pain and itching, at first in her feet and later into her upper thighs and hips. There is also feeling over the abdomen and on her back, and at times tingles running up and down the spine.
▶ She can bend her left leg, and the foot is no longer locked behind the other ankle. She is straighter when sitting up and can cross her ankles.
▶ Gradually she was able to stand, while supported, and push the twisted foot flat on the floor. She can now take a few steps.
▶ Her speech has improved, as the sounds are clearer, and she can put a few words together.
▶ She can push herself upright and hold onto objects.
▶ After two years, Theresa menstruated for the first time since her accident. Her body shape has changed – her breasts have enlarged and her waist is defined.
▶ She developed an awareness of her bladder and can indicate to her mother when she needs to empty it.
▶ She started having intermittent bowel movements, which now occur daily.

Over these past four years there has been a gradual 'rewiring' of nerve connections between the brain and the limbs and organs. Her mother says that Theresa gets quite excited at each sign of progress. Although she is trapped in a life of limited expression, every little change gives her a sense of moving forward.

'Hopeless' nerve damage

When Jack phoned for an appointment, he warned that he would be a challenging case as no one had ever been able to help him. He was so desperate he was willing to try BSR, which he had heard of only recently.

He shuffled into the practice, unable to lift his feet properly, and sat down painfully. At fifty years old, he felt life was no longer worth living. He had virtually lost control of his bowel functions, which was intensely embarrassing. Besides lower-back and sciatic pain, his knees were always aching and often swollen.

His story dated back twenty years, to his time as a paratrooper. He had severely injured his back on a jump, crushing several vertebrae in the lumbar spine. This had caused the spinal nerves to become compressed and damaged, including nerves which connect to the digestive system. As his condition worsened over the years, he consulted orthopaedic surgeons but was told that surgery would be hazardous, and there was a 50 per cent chance that he would end up in a wheelchair.

As the practitioner tested the lower back, he could feel that the muscles throughout the area were rigid, in a protective spasm, and he applied the releases as gently as possible. A week later Jack's arrival at the practice was very quiet – no more shuffling feet. His pain was already much reduced, and he was beginning to regain some control over his bowels. He was so encouraged, he even asked how soon he could play tennis.

Three weeks later, his bowels were functioning normally and he could walk long distances without tiring. The last problem to clear up was the pain in the knees, and he started playing tennis again. He was advised to be careful and to try to avoid any jarring of the spine. As a religious person, Jack described his recovery as a miracle – he had never thought he would walk normally again, let alone play tennis.

Uncovering the body's history

The cells of our bodies store memories. As long as the imprint of a past trauma remains in storage, it holds in place a distortion of the normal flow of life energy, and undermines our well-being, both physically and emotionally.

By the time she was in her late thirties, Helen's long-term lower-back problem was having a negative impact on her life in many ways. After sitting for a while, she was so stiff that she looked like an old woman when she stood up from a chair. She had almost constant diarrhoea, painful menstruation, her legs felt itchy, and she could not lie still in bed at night.

Body stress was released in her lower spine – the area with nerve connections to the digestive and reproductive systems. After several sessions the diarrhoea had lessened, but she still had restless legs and a stiff back on waking.

One day, after a BSR visit, Helen phoned her practitioner to report a startling development. Although no work had been done on her leg, her whole foot and ankle were very swollen, and a huge purple bruise had appeared on her lower leg. Three days later, as the releases were being carried out, she spontaneously remembered an injury that occurred when she was a teenager. In a hockey match, she had been hit with a hockey stick, causing a bruise identical to the present one. On reflection, she realised that had probably been the start of her back condition, as after that she had felt constant leg pain and lower-back stiffness.

As the bruise faded and the foot swelling went down, the various problems gradually withdrew over the next few BSR sessions. Not only did the physical damage of the past come to the surface to heal itself, but this vital piece of her history also rose to Helen's conscious awareness.

A prolapsed spinal disc

Although the expression 'slipped disc' is often used, it is an inaccurate description. The inter-vertebral discs cannot slip, as they are firmly bonded to the surface of the vertebral bodies. However, with incorrect use over time, or as the result of an accident, a compressive force may cause the gel-like centre of the disc to protrude through the fibrous outer cartilage. The resultant bulge, called a prolapsed or herniated disc, may induce pressure on the spinal nerves. The effects may range from pain to loss of sensation to nerve function disorder, leading to muscle weakness and loss of tendon reflexes.

Simon, an engineer aged thirty-five, had pain radiating from his lower back into his groin, and the pain in his right leg was so severe that at times he could not stand on it. He had been forced to give up his sports, running and golf. An MRI scan showed a prolapsed disc in his lumbar spine, and the specialist advised disc surgery. Simon was strongly opposed to having an operation, and decided to try BSR.

His buttock, thigh and calf muscles were extremely tense, as well as his diaphragm, and his back was very sensitive to touch. After the first session, he felt some hope, as the pain started to come and go, and he was aware of tingling in both feet. But he felt worse after the second, with the sensation of electric currents running up and down his right leg. The practitioner assured him that this was a positive sign, indicating that the process of unlocking the stress was under way.

By the fourth session he was completely pain-free. His lower-back muscles felt tight, and he was given an exercise to strengthen his abdominal muscles. After his sixth session he was smiling broadly, as he was able to play golf again. He understood the importance of BSR for health maintenance, and decided to see his practitioner every six weeks.

> Four years later Simon had another MRI scan, and the surgeon was astonished to see no sign of disc prolapse.

Four years later Simon had another MRI scan, and the surgeon was astonished to see no sign of disc prolapse. This demonstrates that, if the stored tension around a prolapsed disc is released, the compression on the disc is relieved. In many cases this allows the pressure on the jelly-like core to be redistributed towards normal. Thus the bulge of the cartilage is reduced and it no longer irritates the spinal nerve.

Myalgic encephalomyelitis (ME)

The casual term for myalgic encephalomyelitis, 'yuppie flu', suggests it is a minor illness, when in fact it may be profoundly debilitating, and continue for years. Viruses or bacteria affect the brain and spinal cord, and a person may experience such weakness and pain that it is impossible to do the simplest task, or even get out of bed.

Angela, aged forty-four, was diagnosed with ME six years ago – her immune system was overwhelmed by previous bacterial infection and glandular fever, which she had as a child. She degenerated to the point of extreme tiredness, and could not even lift her arm to brush her hair. In addition, she had migraines, back pain, aching, burning limbs, and constipation.

The BSR practitioner had to work on her very lightly, as her whole body was intensely sensitive. The immediate response was even more pain, and she was so depressed she had to be encouraged to continue with the process – as her health had been going downhill for six years, naturally it would take time for that to turn around. After the sixth session, she experienced a wonderful week. All the pain and weakness was reduced to the minimum and only the constipation persisted. Over the next three months she continued to improve, except at the time of her monthly period when general severe pain returned.

With her energy level increased, Angela was able to return to work. Three months later her constipation changed to diarrhoea. Then a major emotional release occurred – she confronted the childhood

trauma of a physically abusive father, and dealt with the anger and sorrow she had been suppressing. Nine months after her first BSR session Angela had only slight back pain and headaches at the time of her period. She was able to cope both physically and emotionally with the daunting challenge of emigrating to Australia.

Neck surgery avoided

Imagine being a single mother with a full-time high-pressure career, and virtually losing the use of one arm. Felicity, an accountant in her forties, was facing surgery to fuse vertebrae in her neck. She had less than 30 per cent strength in her left arm, and could no long hold with that hand. Because of the intense pain in her neck, shoulder and upper back, and severe headaches, she was put in traction in hospital for ten days. As there was no improvement, she was told to use a home traction machine for twenty minutes daily. When this made no difference, and surgery was the only option remaining, she turned in desperation to BSR.

The practitioner describes Felicity's back as 'like concrete' from top to bottom. It was clear that lower-back body stress was aggravating her neck problems, even though she was not aware of it. Initially she felt worse after the releases, but she understood when it was explained that her whole spine was in a defensive state, and the muscles would relax by degrees.

By her third session she was excited to feel muscular changes in both her neck and lower back, and said she could not wait to see what the next step in the process would be. At her sixth session she felt exuberant – only tenderness remained in her neck, and her hand had regained 70 per cent of its strength. She felt angry when she thought that she may have submitted herself to unnecessary surgery.

Soon after, 100 per cent function returned to her arm and hand, and her neck pain and headaches were gone.

Felicity's case shows that the spine cannot be dealt with in a fragmented way. It is essential to release compression in the lower back in order for improvement in the neck to occur.

Baby Kara and Hirschsprung's disease

Hirschsprung's disease is a congenital condition in which the rectum and sometimes part of the lower colon have failed to develop a normal nerve network. The area affected cannot expand or make the muscular movements which conduct the contents of the bowel. Therefore waste matter accumulates higher up in the colon and causes distention. The disease is diagnosed by X-ray and by microscopic examination of samples of the bowel wall.

Baby Kara was diagnosed with Hirschsprung's, and at three months old she had severe constipation and abdominal swelling. She was reluctant to feed and vomited frequently. When her distraught mother took her to a BSR practitioner, she had been constipated for over three weeks. The doctors said a colostomy would be necessary – the removal of the lower end of the bowel with an opening made through the abdominal wall for the removal of waste.

The practitioner released body stress on both the mother and the baby, as they were mirroring each other's stress. Later that day the mother phoned, breathless with excitement. Kara had had four large eliminations in the space of six hours.

After three sessions and several monthly maintenance checks, Kara's bowel continued to function correctly. Five years later, she is a normal, healthy, happy child.

How can this miraculous turnaround be explained? As communication was restored to the nerve supply of the digestive system, it is possible that the efficiency of the muscles of the colon above the problem area increased to such an extent that the contents could be propelled through the non-functioning rectal area.

Bladder prolapse

Minor everyday actions – like getting up and sitting down, coughing and laughing – we do them without thinking. But for Eleanor, a woman in her late fifties, these simple things were the source of deep embarrassment, resulting in what she termed an 'accident'. At the slightest exertion, urine leaked from her bladder and she had to wear an absorbent pad, which she changed up to six times a day. She worked in an office surrounded by people, and with her predicament she could never feel at ease.

Two years before she had been diagnosed with a prolapse of the bladder – a sagging due to weakness of the supporting tissues, causing a sensation of constant pressure and incontinence. Now a gynaecologist had scheduled her for surgery in a month's time, to shorten the muscles holding the bladder in place.

Eleanor was deeply unhappy about her situation, but felt reluctant to undergo surgery. When she consulted a BSR practitioner, he explained how nerve compression in the lower back may disturb the efficient functioning of certain muscles and organs. 'Let's go for it,' she said, 'I've got nothing to lose.'

When she returned three days later she was smiling broadly. 'I don't know what it is that you do, but I was fine for two whole days, the best I've been for two years. But today it's been a bit of a problem again.' After two further sessions, the incontinence occurred irregularly, and after the sixth time, she declared herself '60 per cent better'. She decided to postpone the surgery and continue with BSR once a month. Three months later Eleanor was experiencing ten consecutive days free from the bladder problem. After twelve sessions, her lifestyle had returned to normal and her confidence was restored.

Muscle weakness and wasting

Multifocal motor neuropathy is a condition in which there is degeneration of groups of nerve cells in the spinal cord and brain, resulting in muscle weakness and wasting. It gradually worsens and leads to widespread paralysis. The cause is unknown and there is therefore no treatment.

When there is 'no known cause' for a condition, there is the hopeful possibility that the reason for the problem may be body stress undermining nerve function.

Gerry, aged fifty-four, was diagnosed with multifocal motor neuropathy and he felt he had nothing to lose in trying BSR.

He could feel his condition slowly deteriorating, and said that the disease would probably kill him. He had pain and weakness in the legs, lower-back pain, and pins and needles in the feet at times. His arm muscles were so weak that he had to hold his right hand up with his left when he brushed his teeth, shaved or combed his hair.

After the first session he felt an immediate increase in his arm strength, and was no longer supporting one arm with the other. Two months later he had a check-up with his specialist, who was amazed at the strength in his legs. 'Almost back to normal,' she said.

Gerry is continuing with monthly BSR sessions and recently experienced a full week of pain-free living. His arm and leg muscles continue to strengthen.

Carpal tunnel syndrome

A problem in one area may have its source in a completely different part of the body.

Neil, aged forty, owns a sandblasting business, and numbness of his left hand made his work difficult. He was diagnosed with carpal tunnel syndrome, a compression of the median nerve in the wrist area. Surgery was recommended, but he kept putting it off. As he had lower-back and knee pain, he decided to try BSR. After the first session his knee

was more painful and he had sensation coming and going in the numb hand. It became quite painful after the next session, and he started feeling tightness in his neck and shoulders. Finally, after four sessions, his hand felt normal and there was no more pain in his knee. Three years later the hand is still fine, and Neil visits his BSR practitioner whenever he has a very busy period at work, as lifting heavy pieces of glass causes some re-stressing of his lower back. He also finds his energy level improves with regular BSR. A significant extra effect – he has had to invest in new shoes as his feet have gone up a shoe size.

The key to Neil's problems was the lumbar spine. As the compression to the spinal nerves was released, there was improved communication to the legs and feet. With the whole spine developing more mobility, he became aware of the tension stored in his neck area. The nerves supplying the arms and hands emerge from the spine in the lower neck, therefore as the body stress was released, the nerve transmission to his numb hand returned.

At the heart of a three-year-old child

Emily's short life had been marred by health problems. She had had an operation on her trachea when she was two-and-a-half, and she was scheduled for heart surgery at age three, in three months' time.

Her mother's desperate search for something to help her child brought her to BSR. The practitioner describes Emily as very small for her age, thin and weak, with black rings under her eyes. She was afraid of him and refused to lie down on the couch. He had to check her while she sat, wriggling nervously on her mother's lap. Tension was found and released throughout her spine.

Fortunately, at the second appointment, she was willing to sit still, which made it easier to carry out the tests and releases. Her mother reported that Emily's bowel movements were black, sticky and foul smelling. She no longer had dark rings under her eyes.

Three weeks later, on the third visit, she came running up the driveway to the practice. She looked very different, having put on weight. Her mother said her appetite was good. This time Emily was eager to lie down on the BSR couch.

Two months passed before her next session. The little girl who came running in had transformed – she had grown in height, and looked strong and healthy. Her mother shared some wonderful news: Emily had been to the heart specialist for her pre-surgery check-up, and he had decided that the operation was no longer necessary.

> The little girl who came running in had transformed – she had grown in height, and looked strong and healthy.

Tourette's Syndrome

Tourette's Syndrome is a condition that starts in childhood, though the cause is unknown, and becomes chronic. There are involuntary body movements, such as grimaces, jerks and twitches, and compulsive utterances, like grunts or swearing.

For three years, Barry's peculiarities were ignored by his parents until his behaviour in class at school became a problem. He was diagnosed with Tourette's Syndrome at the age of ten. When he was brought for BSR he had neck, arm and leg spasms, and made a continuous 'hic' sound in his throat. Sites of body stress were found mainly in his neck and lower back. Subsequent sessions worked through deeper layers of tension. Then a startling discovery was made. As pressure was applied on two specific sites – one in his upper back, and one in the neck – there was an instant calming effect: the body spasms and the 'hic' ceased.

The practitioner theorised that Barry must have undergone some trauma to this area in the past, although his parents could not recall

any. The releases were carried out once a week until the neck and shoulder area stabilised. After this, his father reported a profound change in Barry. In the school holidays the boy loved accompanying his father on visits to building sites and clients, but previously he was told to wait in the vehicle, as it embarrassed his father to have to explain why he twitched and grunted. Recently, Barry spent the whole day with his father and went into the offices with him – he managed to remain calm with hardly a spasm. The mother's comment regarding the effects of BSR was, 'Already the results are amazing.'

Rewinding to World War Two

As a ten-year-old in London, Betty was a victim of the Blitz. Her house sustained a direct hit by a German bomb, and collapsed on top of the family who were sheltering in the cellar. It took a team of rescuers twelve hours to dig her mother out, and more hours before Betty was found. She was told only weeks later that her six-year-old brother and her grandmother had been killed instantly.

During her fourth BSR session, Betty, now seventy-five, told this story to her practitioner, and asked, 'Do you think this could be affecting my life now, even though it happened so long ago?'

He explained that the body has cellular memory, and traumas may become stored and accumulate. This made sense to Betty, as she had always been highly-strung and had never got over her intense sorrow at losing her little brother. Over many years, she had undergone many forms of treatment to address her problems.

She had lower-back, groin and knee pain, and walking was slow and difficult. At times her neck and shoulders ached. As her right knee was constantly swollen, a specialist had recommended a knee-replacement operation.

After her first BSR session her groin pain escalated, but she said she felt 'a lot better in myself'. As most of the pain eased by the third

visit, she started doing the abdominal muscle exercises her practitioner advised. At each appointment she brought a typed report, headed 'Betty's BSR Diary', noting each change that was occurring.

She now has a BSR check every three weeks. Although she still has knee pain, she says BSR has helped her more than anything else, and her mood is always lighter after the releases.

The 'last hope' for face pain

At thirty-two, Christine had suffered from intense, ongoing facial pain for four years. It dated back to the birth of her child, who had an incurable, terminal condition and required constant nursing. As the wife of a high-profile executive, her life was filled with other stress. She was frequently called upon to play the role of hostess for important clients, and provide gourmet dinners at short notice.

Her GP diagnosed trigeminal neuralgia. This was confirmed by a specialist who recommended a drastic surgical procedure. Certain nerves of the face would be severed, which would terminate the pain, but there was a slight chance of loss of control of the facial muscles. There was another option, which was regarded as somewhat experimental, in which the nerves would be injected with a toxin.

As Christine could no longer tolerate the pain, she was ready to agree to one of the procedures when a friend suggested she give BSR a try first. The practitioner found her neck and shoulder muscles to be rigid and extremely sensitive to the touch. Tension was also stored in her lower spine. Although the areas released ached quite intensely, the facial pain lessened and there were fewer stabbing sensations. By her third session, there was no more pain in her face; she felt only stiffness in her neck and lower back.

At the fourth session, Christine was a changed person. She was cheerful and relaxed, and looked ten years younger. She confided that her last session had brought on an intense emotional release, and she had cried copiously. Somehow she now felt more capable of dealing

with her difficult life situation. Only when she became particularly stressed was she aware of slight facial pain.

Two weeks later there was no trace of the trigeminal neuralgia. She wrote to her specialist to inform him of her amazing recovery, and told him all about BSR, as she felt many people with the same condition could be helped.

Christine has occasional BSR sessions to help her cope with the unremitting stress in her life, and this has prevented the tension from building back up to trigger the facial pain.

Cerebral palsy: a journal of progress

A BSR practitioner writes about Darren:

Darren came to me by good fortune in September as a three-year-old cerebral palsy (CP) boy. His mother had heard about BSR from a friend of hers with a CP child who had had great success with BSR.

Darren was born twenty-nine weeks premature and was on a ventilator too long, which resulted in CP. He is an athetoid spastic – in athetosis there are involuntary writhing movements, especially affecting the hands, face and tongue, therefore the child is unable to speak or use the hands.

When I first saw Darren he could lift his head up while lying on his back, and he had very strong abdominal and neck muscles. His legs were touching together at the knees and the feet were splayed. His hands were clenched fists. His hearing was perfect as was his vision, although his eyes darted a lot in the sockets. He was constipated much of the time. He was also bad-tempered and generally miserable.

After release sessions over the next month, he started rolling himself over onto his tummy and looking around a lot more. He was attempting to leopard crawl around with his arms. For the first time he rolled off the couch and onto the floor and went 'crawl-about'. In November he started 'talking' with sounds and movements of his mouth. He had only ever eaten pureed foods as he choked on solids, even if they were mashed. He threw several tantrums, as his father was away on business a lot, and Darren was upset when he went away.

In December he started having seizures. He had a middle-ear infection and a very high temperature. In January he was very difficult, screaming if he didn't get his way. I think this was his emotional release for the frustration of his situation – he used his voice a lot more. There was a sudden change in March – his eyes no longer flickered and he appeared to be able to focus them. He could now follow movement around.

When his father arrived back from his contract work, he noticed a big change in Darren: he was larger, his eyes were different, he was talking a lot more and crawling along the carpets at home to get around. He had another three seizures.

By May he could say words that his mother could understand – her favourite word was 'mommy', of course. By July his hands started opening up. He no longer always kept his fists closed and he could grip things now and use his hands. He had a few nasty seizures in August and high temperatures. To his mother's surprise she noticed that after a seizure he improved slightly.

In October he started eating solids mashed up. He was constipated at first, then improved. He had no seizures over the first three months of the next year. He was talking much better, with more words and more definition. There was not much improvement in his legs, as he still needed supports to help him stand up, and he did not like standing or practising walking in them.

Now, eight months later, it is nearly two years since his first BSR session, and he has grown like a weed. At five years of age he is fitting into five- to six-year-old clothing. He is observant and loves to be tickled and touched. He thinks accidents of any sort are very funny and will laugh if you trip or bump into something. He loves the sound of his dad's voice. I have seen this special little person develop into a wonderful, bright-eyed child, full of the joys of life. What a privilege.

CHAPTER 19

You may be wondering ...

How to contact a Body Stress Release practitioner

BSR is practised in a growing number of countries around the world, including South Africa, Zambia, England, Scotland, Ireland, Holland, Belgium, Germany, Switzerland, Sweden, Iceland, Australia, New Zealand, Japan, Curacao, Canada and the USA.

There have been several instances of other types of health practitioners attempting to mislead the public by claiming that they also do Body Stress Release, or something very similar. It is important to be aware that BSR is a distinct health-care technique taught only at the BSR Academy in South Africa, on the Garden Route, and it does not form part of any other training.

To locate practitioners go to www. bodystressrelease.com

In addition, there are a few people who trained at the Academy who are no longer members of the BSR Association; they are not registered with or endorsed by the BSR Association, and are not legally permitted to practise any part of BSR. Approved BSR practitioners display the Certificate of Practice, showing the current year, in their consulting rooms, demonstrating that they have fulfilled the continuing education requirements for the year.

How is Body Stress Release regulated?

The Body Stress Release Association was founded in 1987, with a fifty-five page constitution, a legal document by which all practitioners are bound. The purpose of the constitution is to maintain high professional standards of practice, thereby ensuring public safety. It provides a code of ethics, disciplinary powers to deal with misconduct, and a framework to restrict practitioners to functioning within the scope of practice.

In the South African Association the members of the executive committee are elected at the annual general meeting, which forms part of a three-day conference. The committee arranges regional workshops twice a year, as the constitution requires practitioners to attend a minimum of five hours of continuing education per year. The workshops cover theory and technique review, new information and practical experience, thereby providing for the sharing of findings and upgrading of skills. In addition, each year the Academy runs a three-day advanced course for practitioners. The Association newsletter is published three times a year and provides a forum for practitioners, both locally and internationally, to exchange information and views. In other countries these matters are controlled by the association which is formed when there are two or more practitioners resident in the country.

The BSR Association of South Africa is a member of COCHASA, the Confederation of Complementary Health Associations of South Africa. The British BSR Association is a member of the British Complementary Medicine Association and is recognised by the Guild of Holistic Practitioners.

The BSR Academy's Board of Trustees maintains the register of international practitioners, oversees research and is responsible for determining the future development of BSR. Graduates of the Academy receive a registration number from the Board of Trustees, which confers membership of the BSR Association in the country in which they are resident.

How are practitioners trained?

For many years the BSR Academy was situated solely in Rondevlei on the Garden Route of the Western Cape, South Africa. In 2014 a branch of the Academy was opened in England.

The Body Stress Release Academy

A class at the BSR academy

The BSR practitioner training course is an intensive programme, conducted over five months. This may seem a short training period but it has proven to produce graduates who have all the skills necessary to be effective practitioners, and capable of conducting their own practices. The syllabus covers anatomy, the philosophy and principles of BSR, BSR technique theory and practice, client management, communication and a study of the BSR constitution.

The training takes the form of lectures, demonstrations, discussions in small groups as well as presentations by the students to the larger group. In the technique training, once a certain level of knowledge and proficiency is reached the students start practising on a partner.

On successful completion of the course, and after passing both the practical and written examinations, the students fulfil a three-week apprenticeship, attending to clients under the supervision of the Academy faculty. This is a very constructive process, giving the students the opportunity to apply their skills while having a beneficial impact on the health of members of the public. The successful students receive the BSR practitioner certificate at the graduation ceremony.

The Academy class size is limited, as a great deal of individual attention is given to students. The admission requirements are a matriculation certificate and a minimum age of twenty-five, as a certain level of maturity and life experience is required in order to deal with people from all walks of life and in all states of health. Prospective students are interviewed either in person or by telephone before the selection is made.

Body Stress Release students

You may be wondering what types of people are accepted onto the practitioner training course.

BSR practitioners come from a wide range of previous careers. The average age is about forty, as they range from twenty-five to the early sixties. Usually these are people who have found themselves at a crossroads in their life, a time to reassess their purpose. They express the desire to do something meaningful, of benefit to humanity. This may involve leaving a very successful career which no longer fulfils them emotionally or spiritually. People often cite the stress overload of the corporate world as the reason they are willing to make a drastic change in their working life.

BSR practitioners inspire their family members to follow in their footsteps – husbands and wives, parents and children, and brothers and sisters.

As we do not recruit students, those who apply for the course have undergone their own personal BSR journey, and are usually highly committed to pursuing this new career. This dedication is particularly apparent in the case of foreign students, who are prepared to be away from their homes and families while studying, and for many they are willing to undertake the daunting challenge of studying in English, which to some is not their home language.

One year two foreign students evoked great admiration. One from Iceland, the other from Holland, they both had a limited knowledge of English, and did not speak each other's language at all. Every day in their home study time they got together, armed with the Icelandic/English and Dutch/English dictionaries, and laboriously worked their way through the material covered in class that day. They both graduated from the Academy with impressively high marks.

The student experience

Besides training for a new career, the Academy training course provides the student with a rare opportunity. How often in life does an adult find himself or herself in the position of being able to take 'time out', away from the demands and responsibilities of work and family? Students use their free time to enjoy the many activities available in this tourist area – hiking, bird-watching, canoeing on lakes, rivers and sea, as well as many adventure sports.

In addition, most students find themselves undergoing a process of self-development, and discovery of their core selves. With their own body stress being released on a regular basis, they are often able to access and let go of suppressed emotional tensions, resulting in greater self-acceptance and confidence. The wife of a graduate commented that her husband had left home as a grizzly bear, and returned after the course transformed back to the teddy bear she had known at the beginning of their marriage.

The peaceful rural environment is ideal for this time of self-reflection, of reconnecting with those parts of themselves which have been put on hold. The process is enhanced by the support of their fellow students, a group of diverse individuals who are bonded by a common focus. Many graduates describe their time on the course as personally enriching and 'the best five months of my life'. The shared experience leads to the formation of lasting friendships, and the annual conference is a time of joyful reunion with overseas colleagues who fly back to South Africa.

It is a profoundly rewarding experience to train practitioners and observe students mastering the intricacies of BSR. We see them leave carrying the skills in their hands, the specialised knowledge in their minds, and the caring in their hearts, which will enable them to make a contribution to the well-being of other people. The most uplifting result of carrying out the training is receiving phone calls and letters from people who want to let us know how their lives have been transformed by BSR practitioners.

The significance of the BSR logo

The logo depicts a small white leafy tree on a dark green background. Below it, the dark green root system is a symmetrical pattern of loops on a white background. The arcing lines represent the unseen pathways of communication in the body – the coherent flow of life energy. The roots may also symbolise body stress, hidden 'underground', and demonstrate that although stress is an undermining force, it is stored in an organised form (there is order and intelligence, even in apparent chaos). When the stress is released, the life energy is restored, represented by the flourishing tree.

The name Body Stress Release, the logo and the slogan are registered trademarks in South Africa and some other countries.

The slogan that accompanies the logo is: Unlocking tension – Restoring self-healing.

The aims of Body Stress Release

1 *To bring about an improved quality of life.*

How can anyone know the limits of the body's ability to heal and regenerate itself, to function in line with the directions encoded in the blueprint it arrived with? BSR seeks to create an awareness of the potential for well-being that lies within each of us. As the life quality of an individual is improved, so is his or her contribution to the family, to society, and to the world.

2 *To lead people away from the belief that external powers can heal them, and demonstrate that all healing comes from the wisdom within the body.*

This understanding helps to delete the negative programming to which we are all exposed. For example, a woman in her fifties told a practitioner that she suffered from ongoing constipation. 'But of course that's normal for a woman,' she added. A fifty-year-old woman said resignedly, 'I have a difficult old age to look forward to. All the women in my family develop a degenerative muscular disease, so I know it'll happen to me.' It was explained to her that a person may have a predisposition towards a condition, but that it need not manifest if the body is not undermined in its natural ability to self-heal. Twenty years later, at seventy, she has no signs of the dreaded family inheritance.

3 *To serve as a vital component of health-care services, particularly as a basic, first option.*

As body stress is the underlying cause of so many health problems, people can often save themselves time, suffering, and money by being assessed for stored tension before undergoing any invasive procedures. A man in his fifties had pain in his hip joint. He went for a second and then a third opinion, consulting three orthopaedic surgeons in the hope of avoiding surgery. All three made the same diagnosis – a hip-joint replacement was indicated. He turned to BSR, and the pain was reduced after tension was released in his lower spine. After the third session it cleared up entirely. The X-rays of the hip joint must have shown marked wear and tear to convince the surgeons that the solution was surgery. However, it turned out that the source of the pain was compression of lumbar spinal nerves which supply the joint.

What is it all about?

No doubt you have heard the humorous expression, 'Life is what happens while you're making other plans.' Which of the following three scenarios describes the way your life 'happens'?

- *Scenario A:* Every day various stress factors come at you, and you deal with them somehow. You survive, but it feels like being on a treadmill, just getting by but not getting anywhere. *Life is a struggle.*
- *Scenario B:* The stressors in your life seem overwhelming, and you are not coping. Each new difficulty undermines you further, physically, mentally and emotionally. *Life is a downhill slide.*
- *Scenario C:* Each day brings its challenges and you feel you can deal with them. Even though you have some setbacks, you sense that you are growing in strength in all aspects of your being. *Life is an ongoing process of learning and upgrading.*

To aim at living in Scenario C is what it is all about: facing the stress factors, adapting to them constructively, and experiencing an awareness of evolving – in our health, our attitudes, and our capabilities – to a higher level of life expression. Body Stress Release plays a key role in facilitating this evolutionary impulse of life.

Body stress is a simple factor in life, but its undermining effects on life quality may be severe. Body stress is simple to locate and release, but the effects of its release may be far-reaching and profound.

Body Stress Release in a nutshell

Every day we face an onslaught of stress, not only mental and emotional, but also mechanical and chemical. Our bodies are designed to deal with a certain amount of stress, but if it reaches overload level, the body is unable to adapt to it and it becomes stored as tension in physical structures. This may cause pain, stiffness, numbness or postural distortions. In addition, the compression of nerves disturbs the body's communication system and undermines its healthy functioning.

The BSR practitioner carries out a series of pressure tests on the fully-clothed person, and the muscular responses indicate the exact sites of the locked-in body stress. Light but definite pressure is applied in the precise directions indicated. This allows the body to restore its tone, release pressure from nerves and return to its inbuilt ability to heal and maintain itself, and to cope successfully with the stresses of life.

A final mysterious miracle

Bruce, a man of fifty, went to a BSR practitioner because he had pain in his back and shoulders. His body had several deep burn scars from an electrical shock he had suffered many years before. Body stress was located and released throughout his spine. At his second session he was still aching, and some deeper layers of stored tension were dealt with. When he returned three days later he told the practitioner he had experienced a miracle. For the past seven years he had not been able to read a book or the newspaper, as he could not concentrate or remember what he had read. This had caused great difficulty in his day-to-day life.

A friend who knew nothing of his handicap had given him a book for Christmas. After his BSR session Bruce picked up the book and was amazed to find he could read, so he devoured it 'from cover to cover'. He was so excited that his life is normal again, as he can now read anything, concentrate fully, and remember perfectly. He had come to BSR with no expectation that this problem could be solved.

A possible explanation: the electrical shock had disrupted certain nerve pathways in the brain, and induced body stress in the spine. With the release of pressure on nerves, there was a stimulation of some connections to the affected areas of the brain, causing them to be reactivated.

The practitioner's comment: 'Interesting!'

Closing thoughts from Ewald

It is with an overwhelming feeling of gratitude that I reflect back and review the period from that fateful morning when I woke with the shocking realisation that I was paralysed from the waist down. Instantly my world was shattered. That moment in time contrasts dramatically with the experience nine years later when I woke with a total absence of pain for the first time in my life – I thought I had died.

The wisdom gained over the past thirty-five years is that of trusting life and listening to the messages from the body, our most prized possession. It is a sophisticated bio-machine, and has enormous capabilities of self-healing. Coming to this realisation was mind-blowing.

I imagine what Christopher Columbus felt when setting sail – he must have sensed that the prevailing theory of a flat earth was invalid.

My journey into the 'unknown' continues as more and more experiences take place in my body. They expand my field of the 'known' as suddenly the 'unknown' becomes the 'known', thereby releasing fear and enhancing my trust of life.

> We all have this capacity to allow more of the potential within each of us to express itself.

My first three-and-a-half decades of life were spent trying to force my body into submission. Whenever I tried to do something, my body would resist. There appeared to be two of us – me versus a rebellious body. The lesson was that of honouring the biomechanical design of the body. What a joy to go from hating my body to falling in love with it, and knowing that every effect has a cause.

My awareness is enhanced as the layers of stored tension are released, and the communication network improves. We all have this capacity to allow more of the potential within each of us to express itself.

My wish for everyone is that your journey to health may also be wondrous.

INDEX

Page numbers in italics indicate diagrams.

C

D

E

stroke 107
swallowing difficulties 5, 74, 117
swelling 35, 87, 191, 195
sympathetic nervous system 30–31, 32

T

tic douloureux 80
tingling 57, 84
tinnitus 75
tiredness 35, 59, 95, 98, 185–186
    see also myalgic encephalomyelitis (ME)
tongue 5, 80, 127, 202
tooth pain 82
Tourette's Syndrome 199–200
trigeminal neuralgia 80, 201–202

U

upper back 70–74

V

vision 51, 77–78, 170
voice 79, 107, 143
vomiting 51, 127, 149

W

whiplash 20, 40, 75, 76, 78, 186
wrist 40, 53, 83, 84, 197

Y

yuppie flu *see* myalgic encephalomyelitis